Making and Using Turning Tools

Selected Readings from *American Woodturner,*
journal of the American Association of Woodturners

American Association of Woodturners
222 Landmark Center
75 5th St. W
St. Paul, MN 55102-7704
877-595-9094
www.woodturner.org

Contents

3   **Introduction**
The Editors

4   **Using the Spindle Roughing Gouge**
Bob Rosand

8   **Making and Using a Half-Round Tool**
Stacey W. Hager

12   **Make a Skew Chisel**
Bob Rosand

14   **Make a Point Tool**
Stacey W. Hager

16   **Using the Point Tool**
Stacey W. Hager

18   **Making and Using a Cove Tool**
Stacey Hager

21   **Cove Tool Set**
Stacey Hager

23   **Carbide Cutters**
Lyle Jamieson

28   **Getting the Most from Scrapers**
Richard Raffan

33   **Heat-Treating Scrapers**
John Lucas

36   **Negative Rake Scrapers**
Stuart Batty

40   **Make a Plug-and-Inlay Tool**
John Lucas

42   **Making Micro Tools**
Wayne Fitch

46   **Make a Thin-Kerf Parting Tool**
Stacey W. Hager

49   **Making Gouges**
Ed French and John Shrader

52   **Side-Ground Gouge**
Phil Pratt

54   **Making and Using a Hook Tool**
Raul V. Pena

58   **Texture Tool**
Bob Rosand

62   **Golden Dividers**
Bill Smith

Published by American Association of Woodturners,
222 Landmark Center, 75 5th St. W., St. Paul, MN 55102-7704.
877-595-9094, www.woodturner.org.

American Woodturner (ISSN 0895-9005) is published bimonthly
by American Association of Woodturners.

Making and Using Turning Tools
ISBN 978-1-939662-10-1

Printed on Demand in United States of America
American Association of Woodturners, www.woodturner.org

Introduction

Experimenting with turning tools always improves your skill at the lathe, because getting a new tool to work right forces you to slow down and observe closely, deepening your understanding of how tools actually cut wood. You might find that your new tool cuts the wood better than anything else so far, leading to cleaner, quicker turning with less fussing and sanding.

Woodturning tools are surprisingly easy to make. That's because of the fortunate coalescence of several factors: first, most woodturning tools are very simple; second, all woodturning requires sharp tools so all turners must learn how to sharpen; third, if you can sharpen you already know how to shape and put an edge on a length of steel, and finally, wooden tool handles come easily off the lathe. Voila, new turning tools, as close as your lathe and sharpening station.

Making your own tools not only saves you money, it also can help make you a better woodturner. When your investment is low, you can afford to experiment with tool shapes and edge profiles. What you can make won't ever be restricted by the tools you happen to have, because with only a little experience you will become able to make whatever specialized tool you might need, and tune it to cut the wood the way you want.

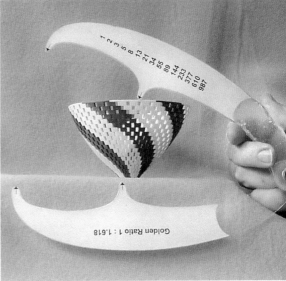

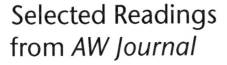

Selected Readings from *AW Journal*

From its founding in 1986, the American Association of Woodturners has published a regular journal of advice, information, and good fellowship for everyone interested in the field. Led by a series of dedicated editors and board members, the *AW Journal* has evolved to become *American Woodturner* magazine, now published in full color six times each year.

The *AW Journal* is a genuine treasure-trove of practical, shop-tested information written by woodturners for their fellow woodturners. *Making and Using Turning Tools* is part of an ongoing series being extracted from this archive. *Making and Using Turning Tools* is available as a 64-page printed book, or as a digital ebook that is readable on all your electronic devices.

Safe woodturning is fun woodturning. A little time spent with this book will help you build strong skills at the lathe while teaching you best woodturning practices.

Using the Spindle Roughing Gouge

Bob Rosand

Next to the small round skew that I use, the spindle roughing gouge (SRG) just might be my favorite woodturning tool.

Most people just use this tool to knock the corners off of stock for spindle turning and then grab other tools. But if sharpened and used properly, the spindle roughing gouge is capable of so much more than that.

In my woodturning shop, I use it for everything from roughing square stock and turning the icicles on my Christmas ornaments to turning Rude Osolnik-style candlesticks. My SRG is perfect for long sweeping curves and for 1/16"-diameter tenons.

Because I primarily work on small-scale projects, I make extensive use of a 1/2" SRG manufactured by Ashley Isles tools. But, the principles are the same for all roughing out gouges whether they be 1-1/2", 3/4", 1/2", or 3/8". Most turners have a 3/4" SRG in their tool kit, and I used one for many years, but my overall favorite is still the 1/2" SRG.

Sharpening

Sharpening the roughing out gouge is really quite easy. But like any other tool, you have to know what you want the finished product to look like before you begin grinding. In the case of the SRG, you want the tool sharpened at about a 45-degree angle. See the tip box "Technique counts for more than tool angle"

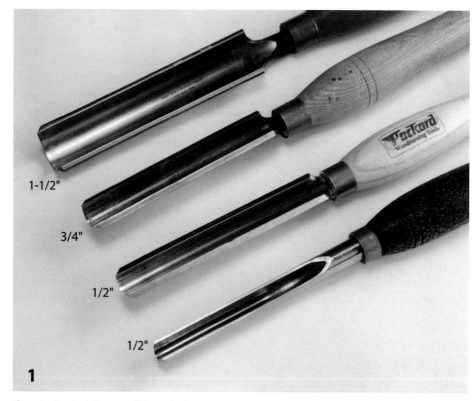

1

If you've limited the use of the spindle roughing gouge to knocking the corners off stock, you're missed some sweet turning experiences. For Christmas ornaments and other small work, I prefer the 1/2" gouge, which is not always easy to find.

about the importance of your grinding angle.

I've met a fair number of people who grind their SRG as though it were a spindle gouge. Experience tells me you lose the effectiveness of the gouge unless it's ground straight across—the straighter the better. If you look at the SRG from the front, you will see that it is horseshoe shaped with a rounded area and two

2

For freehand grinding, use one hand as a fulcrum, then rotate the tool with your other hand. Apply light pressure.

flats. The flats are what I find to be the most useful in my turning.

There are three ways to sharpen the SRG: freehand, on a large platform, and with a sharpening jig.

AW 21:1, p46

3

When sharpening with a large platform, press the tool down with one hand while rotating the tool with the other hand.

4

When using a V-arm with a sharpening jig, use one hand to keep the tool in place and the other hand to roll the tool.

5

Touch the tool to the grinder, then check to see if the angle you selected removed all of the bevel blackened with a felt-tip marker.

Freehand. Most grinders include a standard platform (about 1×3") that locks in front of the wheel. If this describes your platform, you can still sharpen the SRG on it with practice. When I sharpen using this method, I create a fulcrum with my fingers.

As shown in *Figure 2*, place one hand on the tool rest and the tool on top of your hand. With your other hand, hold the tool and rotate it while grinding.

Now, lower the tool handle, touch the tool to the wheel, then raise the handle until you are sharpening the bevel—not the edge.

When I started turning, I never quite grasped the idea of sharpening the bevel and not the edge, but it's really quite simple when you think about it. If you sharpen the bevel, the bevel will always remain the same. But if you sharpen the cutting edge, you slowly change the bevel, making the tool angle blunt and unusable until you regrind a new bevel. Save yourself time at the grinder and learn to sharpen the bevel.

Large platform. You may be fortunate enough to own a grinder with a platform about 3×5". If so, sharpening the SRG is easier. Adjust the platform so that its angle approximates the 45-degree bevel. Now, place the SRG on the platform. With your thumb or fingers, hold it flat on the platform and rotate the tool with the other hand (*Figure 3*).

Here's a reliable way to test that the platform angle is correct. Mark the SRG with a felt-tip marker, then touch the tool to the grinder. If you have a parallel shiny grind line, the angle is perfect. If the mark resembles a little triangle, adjust the platform up or down. I usually do this by tapping my tool handle on the platform.

Sharpening jig. Some turners prefer to sharpen with a jig such as the Wolverine jig. Actually, I'm kind of spoiled and do most of my sharpening using a jig. This jig system includes a V-arm that adjusts in or out (*Figure 4*).

Place your SRG in the V-arm pocket and make a rough setting. Use the felt-tip marker method described earlier, then touch the tool to the grinder. As with the platform method, a parallel grind line tells you that the setting is perfect. Got a triangle marking on the grind? Move the V-arm in or out until you nail a perfect angle. Now, sharpen the bevel (*Figure 5*).

With all of these methods, a light touch of the tool to the grinding wheel is all that is required. Once you have established the desired bevel, you only want to touch it up at the wheel.

If you generate a lot of heat when sharpening, you are pressing down too hard. Unless I am changing the bevel angle of a tool, I use little or no downward pressure when sharpening.

5 ways to put the spindle roughing gouge to use

The simplest use of a spindle roughing gouge is to true up a cylinder. That is to take a square block of wood and make it round. If I think back to my days as a fledgling turner, this was a major accomplishment. Here are some tips to help you master this tool.

Technique counts for more than tool angle

That bevel on your spindle roughing gouge should be at about 45 degrees; anywhere from 48 degrees to 42 degrees is acceptable. More important is how you use the tool: Lower the tool handle, rub the bevel, then slowly raise (pivot) the handle until it starts to cut. Think about this routine every time you take a cut until it's second nature to you.

If the angle is a degree or two from 45 degrees, it will make no difference in your cut. Technique does matter.

When you turn with an SRG, the wood grain should run parallel to the bed of the lathe, not perpendicular as though it were a bowl.

The SRG was not designed for and will not work well for roughing out or turning bowls. Don't even think about it! See the tip box "Let's get it right" for more details.

Roughing cylinders. When you rough down a cylinder, place the tool on the tool rest, point the flute of the tool in the direction you intend to cut, rub the bevel (not cutting yet), then slowly raise the handle until the tool begins to cut. That will give you the proper cutting angle. If you do this each and every time you approach the wood, it will soon become second nature to you, and eventually you will not think about it.

Trueing stock. You can then begin to true up the stock you are working on. When you move the tool toward the headstock, point the flute in that direction. When you are cutting toward the tailstock, point the flute in that direction. You will eventually develop a rhythm to cutting *(Figure 6)*.

Smooth tool rest. Take a few minutes and closely examine your tool rest. If it has lots of nasty nicks and dings in it (from other turners, obviously not from your work), you need to remove them with a file and 220-grit sandpaper.

These nicks will translate directly into your work. Another little trick that will keep the tool moving along the tool rest is to occasionally rub the rest with a chunk of paraffin wax (available where canning supplies are sold). If the wax builds up, simply clean it off with your fingernail and reapply fresh wax.

Shaping. If you intend the cylinder you turned earlier to become a weed pot, the SRG can be helpful. I use a spindle gouge to shape the body of the weed pot, but I rely on the SRG

When trueing a cylinder, point the tip of your spindle roughing gouge toward the tailstock, as shown in the photo. Rotate the tip toward the headstock when you true in the opposite direction.

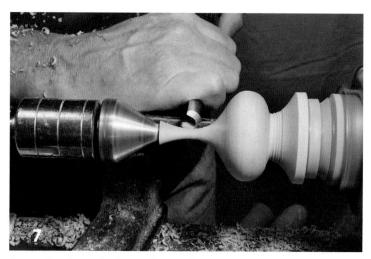

For turning the neck of a weed pot, roll your spindle roughing gouge on its side. This tool isn't designed for turning tight curves, but is excellent for long, sweeping curves.

1/2" spindle roughing gouge: Hard to find

Most woodturning catalogs sell standard spindle roughing gouges. However, the 1/2" SRG is a bit harder to find. Packard Woodworks (packardwoodworks.com) sells a 1/2"-wide version of the 3/4" SRG. My favorite is the Ashley Isles round-bar style. One U.S. source is Tools for Working Wood (toolsforworkingwood.com).

If you buy the tool with a handle, I highly recommend knocking off the factory handle and making a new one at least 2" longer. This will increase the leverage of the tool, and it will work much better for you.

—Bob Rosand

For delicate work like the icicle segments of a Christmas ornament, turn the spindle roughing gouge on its side. With a soft touch, you can complete this piece supported only by the chuck (no tailstock).

How small? With a 1/2" spindle roughing gouge turned on its side, you can turn these 1/16×3/8" ebony perches for ornamental birdhouses.

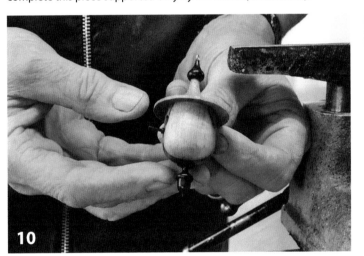

The details of this acorn birdhouse were turned with a spindle rouging gouge.

Let's get it right: It's a SPINDLE roughing gouge

Roughing gouge? Gives us the shivers. Roughing-out gouge? Also wrong.

Nick Cook, Alan Lacer, and Bob Rosand are among the many woodturning teachers who agree that the terms roughing gouge and roughing-out gouge are big problems. Some new woodturners—left to their own devices—believe they can attack bowl stock with this tool. Not true! Worse: It's dangerous!

This is a tool for spindle work only. Please join our campaign to attach the correct name onto this tool: spindle roughing gouge.

The 1-1/2" and 3/4" tools are probably better suited for rough work, but you can accomplish a lot of detail work with a 3/4" and 1/2" SRG. As with any other tool, all it takes is practice and an effort to learn the tool's capabilities.

to shape the neck of the weed pot. In *Figure 7*, I am doing just that. You can use the spindle gouge to do this shaping, but the spindle roughing gouge does it better. Note that the tool is very much on its side, and I am taking advantage of the flat areas of the SRG to make a nice smooth neck on the weed pot.

Delicate work. I also turn delicate work—like the icicles on my Christmas ornaments—with an SRG. As shown in *Figure 8*, the turning stock is clamped in a spigot-jaw chuck and is not supported by the tailstock.

Turn the SRG on its side, taking advantage of the flat area. I turn about 90 percent of the entire icicle with an SRG before cleaning up the shape with a 1/4" round skew or 1/2" skew. If I had ground the SRG back as though it were a spindle gouge, I could not have accomplished this.

Despite its name, this tool is capable of refined work. *Figures 9 and 10* show a 1/16 × 3/8" ebony scrap being turned for an acorn birdhouse. I turned this detail with my 1/2" SRG rolled on its side. With a light touch and a sharp tool, you, too, can accomplish this.

You can produce the same work with a parting tool or skew laid on its side, but the SRG—especially when properly sharpened—does it much better.

Bob Rosand of Bloomsburg, Pennsylvania, is a professional turner and educator and frequent contributor to American Woodturner.

Making and Using a Half-Round Tool

Stacey W. Hager

The half-round tool is a traditional spindle tool that has been around woodturning shops for centuries. It is easy to make, simple to sharpen, and performs just about every cut required in spindle work.

This tool combines some of the properties of a spindle gouge and a skew. However, its cutting action is a little different than that of either the gouge or skew. If you are having trouble with tear-out on beads or coves in a particular piece of wood, give this tool a try. My experience is that the half round tool often performs well on extremely, dense, brittle woods such as ebony and blackwood *(Figure 1)*.

Steel options

I often use discarded reamers and drill bits for my homemade tools, but you must be sure to test the end you plan to sharpen with a file to make sure it is hardened. (If the file skates across the surface, the steel is hardened. If the file digs in, the steel is soft.)

For this tool, I used an old reamer shaft. The shaft was hardened to about 5/8" behind the flutes. I removed the flutes by grinding four deep notches just below the neck (in the top of the flutes). I then clamped the flute end in a vice and snapped it off. High cobalt tools are often hardened throughout their length.

The chuck end of most tools is left soft to reduce brittleness and

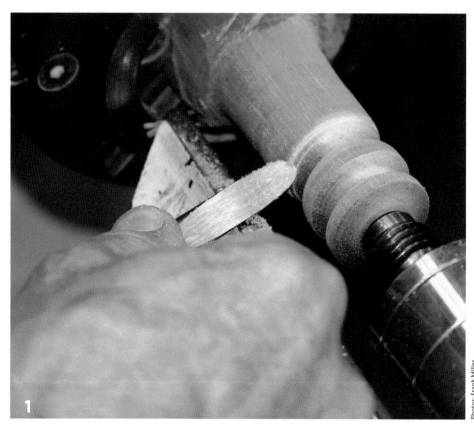

When your spindle work demands fine detail and a clean cut, call on the half-round tool to finesse the job.

to allow a better grip in a chuck. If you cut off the flutes, the adjacent portion of the shaft is usually hardened for a short distance.

You may find pre-hardened 01, W1, A2, or M2 precision drill blanks or M7 Dixie Pins (6" lengths) at machinist supply companies such as Enco, Dixie Industrial Supply, and MSC. The blank diameter could be from 1/16" to over 1", but 3/8" is usually most versatile. Dixie (dixiepins.com) sells Special Decimal Diameter Dixie Pins in 6" lengths

and diameters from .0001–.9887. (All pins are hardened to Rockwell 62–63 and ground to tolerance +.0005– .0000 in.)

Grind the flat

Remove excess steel by grinding with a coarse stone. (I use a standard 1×8" 36-grit wheel.) With the grinder stopped, rest the blank against the tool rest and the grinding wheel so that the wheel contacts the rod 1/2" to 3/4" below what will become the tip of the tool.

Photos: Frank Miller

AW 21:3, p44

With a permanent marker, make a reference line around the blank where it contacts the tool rest. Use this line to help you return to the same grinding position. Now, grind a flat on the rod to half its thickness. Quench often in water. If the steel hisses, you need to quench sooner *(Figure 2)*.

Use a dial caliper to help you grind exactly to the center of the rod. Measure the diameter and divide by two to get the thickness you are shooting for *(Figure 3)*.

Stop grinding .005 –.010" before you get to depth and carefully slide the tool down the rest to continue the flat out to the tip.

Avoid rounding over the tip. You may wish to switch to an 80-grit wheel with an adjustable tool rest to make this step easier. To set this up, place the cove you just ground against the stopped wheel and adjust the tool-rest table until it is flat against the rod. Then slide the rod down the tool rest and continue the flat grind to the end.

Grind the bevel

To remove metal, shape the bevels by hand on the coarse stone. Your goal

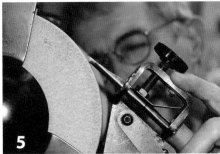

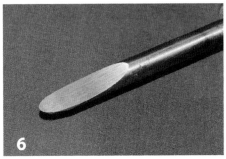

should be a 45-degree tip bevel angle and an 80-degree included side bevel angle. Eyeball each angle and grind a flat. Measure what you get and adjust as necessary *(Figure 4)*.

If you use a jig, set the side angle first by moving the V-arm in or out. Then, set the tip angle by loosening the wing nut and moving the articulated head. Note: One

adjustment changes the other, so check back and forth until both are right on. I use a bright light and sight across the surface of the wheel toward the light, increasing or decreasing gaps between the wheel and the tool surface until I get the desired angle *(Figure 5)*.

Once the angles are set, grind the bevels. Use a light touch until you achieve a nice symmetrical fingernail shape. Be sure to continue the grind around the sides until the rod is almost parallel to the surface of the wheel. This gives you long wings, which can be used like a skew *(Figure 6)*. The tip profile should be a gentle (not quite round) parabola. Finally, shorten the bevel to about 1/8" by grinding a secondary bevel *(Figure 7)*.

This grind corresponds to that of a standard spindle gouge. If you wish to use this tool for detail work, you may want to change the tip angle to 35–40 degrees and the side angle to about 70 degrees. This tip profile should be a narrow, fairly pointed ellipsoid. (The radius at the point may be as little as 1/32".)

This shape is great for tight places—perfect for tiny coves and the V between adjacent beads. The compromise is catchiness. With this grind you must make light cuts and maintain constant bevel contact.

Finesse, finesse, finesse!

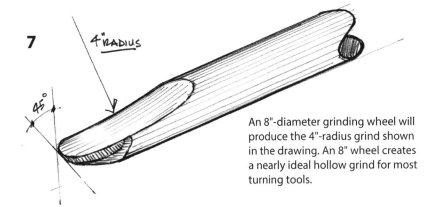

An 8"-diameter grinding wheel will produce the 4"-radius grind shown in the drawing. An 8" wheel creates a nearly ideal hollow grind for most turning tools.

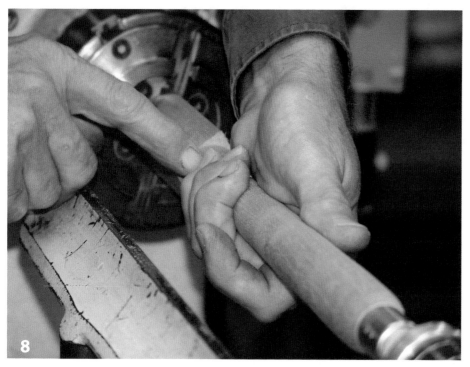

8

9

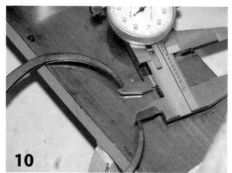

10

Turn the handle

Size the tool handle for your body. For this tool, I like a handle length that reaches from the inside of my elbow to the break of my wrist (about 9" for me). This should allow the handle to swing past your body comfortably. If you have a pear-shaped physique, you may want to make the handle shorter.

I chose crepe myrtle, a medium-density wood, for this handle.

The diameter should be such that your middle finger will barely touch your hand's heel when wrapped around the smallest part of the handle (about one-fourth of the distance from the end) as shown in *Figure 8*.

I like the handle to swell gently until the thickest part is beneath my middle finger when I wrap my hand around the handle just below the ferrule. At this point, my middle finger is about 1/8" from touching the palm.

Unless you need the strength, I feel that bulkier handles make it more difficult to rotate a tool smoothly. British woodturner Allan Batty recommends pointing your index finger along the tool to enhance control.

First, drill the hole for the tool. Clamp the 1-1/4×1-1/4×13" stock in a chuck using the tailstock to center the opposite end. Rotate the handle at a low speed and back out the tailstock center. If the centerpoint wobbles, loosen the chuck, apply a little tailstock pressure, and retighten the chuck. If this does not get rid of the wobble, you may need to round down to a flat near the tailstock end and use a steady rest.

Once the blank is centered and rotating smoothly, replace the live center with a chuck and drill a hole 2–3" deep for the tool. I measure the tool with dial calipers and choose a bit that is .001 or .002 smaller. (In dense hardwood, you may have to drill the exact size.) A set of numbered, lettered, and fractional drill bits with a decimal equivalents chart is handy. You'll often find 115-piece bit sets on sale for under $40 in tool catalogs. The charts are usually free at machinists' tool supply companies.

Place a small cone on your live center and begin turning your handle by rounding the blank to about two-thirds the length of the handle. Make your blank 2–3" longer than you want your handle. This keeps your turning tools safely away from the chuck when you finish the far end.

Add a ferrule

Stainless-steel or brass tubing, brass compression fitting nuts, or brass oxyacetylene hose ferrules are ideal for handles. For this project, I chose an oxyacetylene hose ferrule purchased at a hardware store.

To fit the ferrule, measure the inside diameter of the ferrule with dial calipers or inside calipers (*Figure 9*). Transfer this measurement to outside calipers by adjusting them to just skim over the inside caliper blades or points (*Figure 10*).

Next, turn a tenon for the ferrule; I use a bedan. Begin at the tailstock end and check for a snug fit as you reduce the stock. If you use your dominant hand to make a peeling cut, you can hold the calipers in your other hand. (I do not use dial or vernier calipers for this job because I find them too grabby

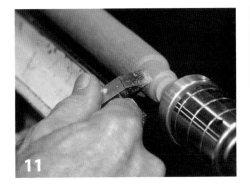

for one-handed turning.) Reduce the diameter until the calipers slip over the tenon easily. Check the fit, adjust as necessary, move up the tenon, and repeat until the tenon matches the length of the ferrule, plus about 1/8" *(Figure 11)*. If your ferrule has a reduced neck, you may need to turn a second smaller tenon. I like to make this second tenon protrude about 1/8" past the ferrule and trim it later *(Figure 12)*. Press the ferrule into place. The fit should be snug but not overly tight, as it will tighten more as the tool steel is driven in.

To finish the fitted ferrule, sand with 600- to 1200-grit wet or dry sandpaper or fine crocus cloth. Follow this with a polishing compound and either wax or clear lacquer. Mask the ferrule to protect the finish.

With the ferrule in place, shape the handle, sand, and apply finish if you wish. I like the feel of raw wood, although a little wax and/or oil may help keep the handle cleaner and avoid attracting grime.

To mount the tool in the handle, bevel the end to remove sharp edges. Start the tool in the hole by hand.

Drive the tool home by striking the butt of the handle on a piece of soft wood supported by a heavy workbench or concrete floor.

Put the tool to use

Unlike a spindle gouge, you can plunge this tool straight in and work it back and forth to quickly shape a cove. You can then turn the tool up on edge (starting with the flat side vertical) and scoop out the cove to its final shape as you would with a spindle gouge.

Remember to aim the bevel in the direction you want the cut to go. The final cut surface is usually clean and smooth *(Figure 13)*.

Roll this tool over on its side and lead with the handle, and you get a skew-like push or pull cut at about 10 o'clock or 2 o'clock from the tip. For this cut, rub the bevel. The flat ground surface should be about halfway between vertical and horizontal, and the cutting edge should be skewed about 45 degrees to the axis of the wood.

This is a handy cutting tool to use on long shallow coves, in tight

places, or when you just don't want to reach for a skew chisel.

Stacey Hager is a member of the Central Texas Woodturners Association of Austin. He has been a frequent contributor to American Woodturner *magazine.*

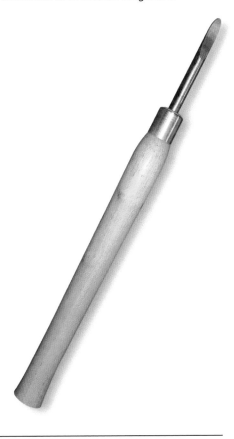

Make a Skew Chisel

Bob Rosand

I make my living mostly by turning small gift items that I sell at local craft fairs and consignment galleries. My best sellers include Christmas tree ornaments, pens, ring holders and bottle stoppers.

As I became more experienced at producing these spindle-turned items, I found that I was relying on fewer and fewer tools to do the job. One of the tools that I can't do without is a small round skew.

I don't remember how I discovered this skew. At one time I purchased 1/4 in. x 1/4 in. x 8 in. bars of high speed steel from Enco manufacturing and turned them into skews for my Christmas ornaments. They worked OK, but it took more time than I wanted to soften the square edges so that they would roll on the tool rest and not bruise it. Then I read something about round and oval skews. I went to my trusty Enco catalog and, lo and behold, discovered 8-in. lengths of 1/4-in. round high-speed steel. I purchased a few, made round skews, and have been using them ever since.

After seeing me use the tool turners often wanted to buy them, so I started demonstrating this simple tool-making process along with my techniques for ornaments and other small items. Here I'll describe the process for a round 1/4-in. skew. I am often asked about larger round skews, usually 3/8 in. or 1/2 in., but I do not use them because they seem a bit heavy and cumbersome for my purposes. When I need a larger skew, I switch to my standard 1/2-in. rectangular skew and am very happy with that.

The author's handy round skew, above top, looks like one straight from a catalog.

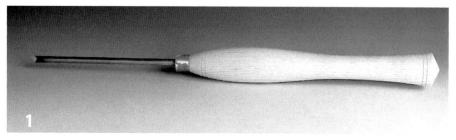

The round skew is shop-built from readily available materials: a maple blank, a steel shaft and a section of copper pipe.

Photos by Bob Rosand

If you are going to make a round skew, you'll need a handle. When I conduct workshops, I am often surprised both by the number of people who have never made their own handles and also by the variety of handle shapes they come up with after I finally get them to make their own handles.

Making a handle

The handles that I make are generally maple, ash, cherry or oak. I start with a blank about 10 in. long by about l-1/2 in. square. The finished handles are not heavy in cross section. I keep them light because I consider this skew a finesse tool.

I mark out the centers and then chuck the handle blank between the headstock and tailstock of the lathe and use a roughing-out gouge to bring the blank to a cylinder.

Designing the handle is up to you. I prefer simple, comfortable shapes. You'll need to turn a tenon on one end of the blank to accept a metal ferrule to reinforce the handle and prevent splitting. If you are unsure of what shape to make the handle, copy the one shown here or duplicate the handle of one of your favorite tools.

Begin by marking the length of the ferrule on the handle blank and put the metal piece aside. For a skew this size a 1/2-in. section of copper pipe with an internal diameter of 1/2 in. works well.

Lay your regular 1/2-in. skew flat on the tool rest and use it as a peeling tool to bring the tenon that will accept the ferrule close to

AW 16:2, p37

After roughing out the blank to a cylinder, use a skew in a peeling motion to form the tenon for the tool ferrule.

Refine the shape of the handle with a spindle roughing gouge, smooth it with a skew, and then use the point of the skew to shape the bottom of the handle

The first step in sharpening the skew is to create a screwdriver shape on the shaft.

Grind at an angle to form the skew.

the diameter of the interior of the ferrule. I use my vernier calipers to determine the interior diameter of the ferrule and then transfer that to the tool handle. If you are unsure about using the skew to size the tenon, a parting tool will work fine. Once you have a snug fit tap the ferrule into place, return the blank to between centers and continue turning your handle. I use my spindle roughing gouge to shape the rest of the handle and then make a final cut or two with the skew, followed by sanding up to about 400 grit.

At this point you need to drill a 1/4-in. diameter hole to accept the shaft of the tool. I do this on my lathe after fitting the bit in a chuck mounted in the headstock.

I drill this hole 2 in. deep. This leaves me 6 in. of usable skew. I find

that the round skews on the market have tool shafts that are altogether too short. If the steel doesn't fit snugly into the handle, I mix up a bit of five-minute epoxy and glue the shaft into place and allow to dry.

Making tool handles is great practice for the novice. You lose very little if you manage to destroy the tool blank.

A distinctive handle also makes it easier to identify your tools under all those chips and you will save a few bucks if you buy your tools unhandled.

Sharpening the skew

Now the tool needs to be sharpened. The first step is to make a screwdriver out of the round steel shaft. To do this I support the shaft of the tool with my fingers, which I rest on the

tool rest. The tool is 90° to the wheel. I grind each side alternately until it looks like a screwdriver. Then I grind the skew angle into the tool.

Once the angle is established, I grind each side alternately, but at about a 30°-to-35° angle until I am satisfied with the grind. To me, the angle is not critical—a couple of degrees one way or another does not affect how the tool works.

As the tool gets hot, avoid quenching it in water to cool it. I have been told by those who know that high-speed steel tends to fracture when cooled in water. I haven't had any problems along these lines, but why tempt fate?

Bob Rosand is a professional turner and demonstrator in Bloomsburg, PA, and a frequent contributor to the AW *Journal.*

Make a Point Tool

Stacey W. Hager

Whenever I need to finesse a bead in a tight spot, I always grab my point tool. Why? The sharp point shines in executing detail work. And best of all, it's virtually catch-free.

I've found the point tool to be an extremely versatile scraper for many turning tasks. Because the 120-degree angled faces produce relatively obtuse cutting edges, it makes shear cuts and scrapes easy to control.

Follow these steps to make your own point tool and get started using it.

Grind the steel

To make your own point tool, you need a 6"-long piece of high-speed steel (HSS) hardened to Rockwell 62 or 63. One source is Carbide Products Inc., www.dixiepins.com. A steel rod 1/4" to 5/16" in diameter is ideal; my favorite tool stock is 9/32".

Start by chucking the rod in Stronghold #1 jaws or something similar and mark the center in one end with a small combination drill/countersink held in a drill chuck mounted in the tailstock. This dot will serve as a center reference as you grind the faces. (A carbide bit or diamond stylus marks better on HSS.) All you need is a tiny dot (about 1/32" deep), but it must be able to survive a lot of grinding *(Figures 1, 3)*.

Hollow-grind three angled faces on one end of the rod to form a three-sided pyramid. Each face should form an angle of

approximately 25 degrees with the centerline. The functional range is from 20 degrees to 30 degrees (more acute is hard to control, more obtuse does not cut well). Space the faces equally around the rod at 120 degrees. You can grind the faces by hand or use jigs, but each face must be the same length and at the same angle *(Figure 2)*.

I begin roughing out the point by hand. Then I make a temporary handle (a dowel with a hole in it) and use a Wolverine-type arm to hold the tool at a constant angle for the finish grind. If you don't trust your eye, build a jig as shown in *Figure 5*.

Grinding notes

If you grind by hand, make a mark around the rod where it contacts

the tool rest. This mark helps you position the tool at the same angle for each grind. Grind the faces a little at a time, trying to keep them equal. A small equilateral triangle should form around the center dot. Use this triangle to help you keep the faces equal.

After you get three faces ground at approximately 120 degrees, an edge of the pyramid should always point straight up as you grind the face opposite. Continue grinding alternate faces until they form a point.

With a Sharpie pen, mark an even line around the rod a little more than one diameter away from the tip. Spin the rod in a chuck, then steady the pen on the tool rest as shown in *Figure 4*. Use this line to keep the

AW 20:3, p32

"scallops" formed by grinding the same length. Grinding the scallops to a line 110 percent of diameter down from the tip will produce a face angle of about 25 degrees. If all three faces are ground at the same angle and the scallops are the same length, your point will be centered.

Do not quench extremely hot tool steel. If it sizzles, it's too hot. Doing so may cause micro fractures, which can damage the surface and reduce the edge quality and longevity. To prevent this, use a heat sink. I use two 1/2×4×6" pieces of aluminum to "sandwich" hot tools. This draws the heat out almost as quickly as water without the mess or damage. Try taping the back edges together so the aluminum pieces open like a book. Simply place the hot tool on the bottom piece and close the book.

You can make a 120-degree indexing wheel by drawing a 3" circle on a block of wood and dividing the circumference into thirds as shown in *Figure 5*. Draw a line from the center to each dividing point. Drill a perpendicular hole, the diameter of the rod, through the exact center. Press the wheel onto the rod. Grind each face with one of the lines pointing straight up. You could also drill a hole through the exact center of an equilateral triangle, and use a level or table to ensure that each face is at 120 degrees *(Figure 6)*. A protractor such as the General model no.17 is handy for checking the face angles. I recommend a dial caliper for measuring the diameters and lengths.

Turn a handle from a dense wood (ebony or boxwood are two good choices) so that most of the tool's weight will be in your hand. The handle should be about 6" long and around 1-1/8" in diameter at the widest point. Your middle finger should just reach the heel of your hand when stretched around the narrow end.

Stacey Hager is a member of the Central Texas Woodturners Association of Austin. He has been a frequent contributor to American Woodturner *magazine.*

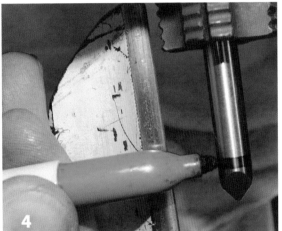

Figure 3. Mark the center of your high-speed steel with a carbide bit or diamond stylus.

Figure 4. Use a Sharpie marker to guide your formation of three equal sides.

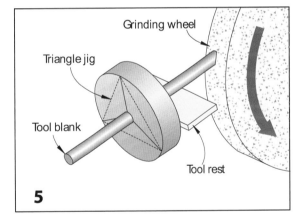

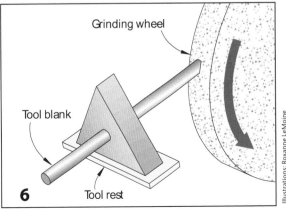

Illustrations: Roxanne LeMoine

Using the Point Tool

Stacey W. Hager

The point tool is used for both spindle and faceplate work. It is also useful for details such as texturing and making designs in the bottom of bowls and hollow forms. I find myself picking this tool up in dozens of situations where I need access and don't want to risk a catch with a detail gouge or the point of a skew.

This is a finesse tool, not a hogging tool. The point tool really shines on delicate, high-definition spindles such as finials, boxes, clock parts, and chair parts. It was originally used on small objects made of ivory, bone, or on extremely dense, fine-grained hardwoods such as ebony or boxwood. There are four basic cuts that can be performed with this tool: The V-groove, the bead, the facing cut, and the planing cut.

V-cut

Use the V-cut for detailing and as the beginning step in forming a bead. Examples of detailing are the signature lines in the bottom of a bowl or vase and the delicate line marking the transition between flats and beads in spindle work. V-cuts are also a fast, efficient, and controllable way to produce texture.

To make a V-cut, place the point tool on the tool rest perpendicular to the surface of the wood. Rotate the handle until a triangular face is up. Drop the handle until this cutting face is almost horizontal. Push the tool straight in as shown in the photo *V-cut*.

Bead

There are two classic bead shapes: Greek (elliptical) and Roman (semi-circular). Begin either by making a V-cut. For a semi-circular bead, the V-cut depth should be about one-half the width of the bead. For the elliptical shape, the V-cut must go a little deeper.

To scrape a bead, simply make a V-cut and swing the handle toward the center of the bead keeping the triangular face horizontal. Pulling the handle back slightly allows the edge to follow the curve without the point touching the adjacent side of the V-groove. Repeat for the other side.

To cut a bead, make a V-cut and begin swinging the handle very slightly toward the center of the bead. This pulls the point out of the groove so that it will not catch the opposite side. Drop the handle as you roll the tool slightly away from the bead. This brings up the cutting edge and rotates the bottom face toward the bead. This lower triangular face should float over the newly cut surface acting as the rubbing bevel. This face starts out almost vertical and ends up horizontal. You are rolling the bead uphill from the V-cut rotating the tool toward the center of the bead as you progress (like a windshield wiper with a twist). Control the cut by varying the amount you drop and roll the handle. Reverse these motions to cut back downhill.

Allan Batty recommends pointing your index finger along the tool for increased fine motor control. If you are right handed and are rolling the right hand side of a bead, you need to place this "pointing finger" along the right side

V-cut: With a triangular face up, push the tool straight into the stock between centers.

AW 20:3, p34

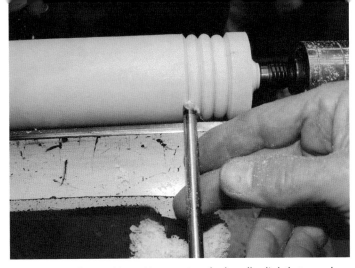

Bead step 1: After making a V-cut, swing the handle slightly toward the center of the bead.

Bead step 2: Drop the handle slightly as you roll the bead "uphill."

Facing cut: On an end-grain surface, align one triangular face with the surface. Drop the handle, then arch the cut toward the center.

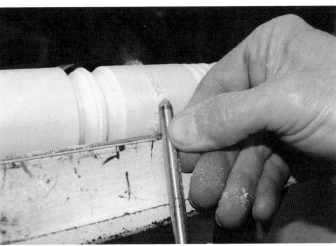

Planing cut: Place the triangular face of the tool flat on the surface. Advance the handle slightly in the direction of the cut.

of the tool so your hand can rotate from vertical to horizontal as you roll the bead upward. For the left side of a bead you would start with the "pointing finger" on top of the handle so you can rotate smoothly to the right as you go from the V-groove to the top of the bead. Everything is just the opposite for us lefties.

One advantage of this tool is that you can move back and forth (both uphill and downhill) over a surface until you get the shape you want. This is the only tool I am aware of that will cut uphill on a bead. As you would expect, the downhill cut is smoother. The usual practice is to rough one side of the bead going uphill from the beginning V-groove, then to refine and finish with a downhill cut. Repeat this procedure for the other side of the bead.

As with any complex cut, practice may be necessary to get all of this coordinated. I recommend practicing on a nice green branch until you get the hang of it. Begin with beads about the diameter of the tool. The challenge is to make smaller and smaller beads.

Facing cut

Align one triangular face of the tool with the surface you wish to face off (usually an end grain surface). Drop the handle until the upper cutting edge is almost horizontal. Push the cut straight in, arcing the point of the tool toward the center of the spindle. This should produce a cut almost as clean as the skew with less chance of a catch.

Planing cut

This is useful in tight places where you can't access with a skew or gouge (for example, the flat separating a cove and a bead). Make this cut by placing one triangular face of the tool flat on the surface to be planed. Advance the handle slightly in the direction of the cut and push the tool along the surface. The cutting edge should be about 45 degrees from vertical or horizontal. Try to maintain a slight feather or fuzz in front of the cut. As with a skew, keep the cut at the heel of the cutting edge (away from the point).

Stacey Hager is a member of the Central Texas Woodturners Association of Austin. He has been a frequent contributor to American Woodturner *magazine.*

Making and Using a Cove Tool

Stacey Hager

Have you ever wrecked a beautiful spindle putting that final little cove in the flat between two beads? Have you spent 10 minutes or more with a gouge trying to adjust both sides of a cove into symmetry? Boy, have I got a tool for you.

The cove tool is easy to make by grinding one end of a round steel rod at an angle of about 40 degrees. Round rods of hardened tool steel are not difficult to obtain, so you can make cove tools in any convenient size from smaller than 1/4" up to about 1/2". This little tool will make you wonder why you ever turned a cove any other way. I still prefer to use a gouge on 1" and larger coves, but this tool is unbeatable for delicate finial work and in dense, hard, fine-grained woods such as ebony or boxwood.

Notes from a cove-tool fan

This tool became widely accepted in the trades because it was economical to make, easy to sharpen, and fast and efficient at its task. I first learned to use the cove tool from English turner Allan Batty. Here are a few suggestions to improve handling of this tool.

- The smaller tools are excellent for making the petite cove at the base of a bowl or box. This cove produces "lift" by making a shadow line between the base or foot and the surface upon which it rests.
- Each cove tool behaves differently. You may have to experiment to find the blade's "sweet spot."
- The cove tool should cut more than it scrapes, particularly in dense, fine-grained woods.
- Maintain a sharp edge. Rough spots in a turned cove indicate dull areas on the blade.

Turn a handle

You can turn your handle from any hardwood. My favorites are ebony, maple, cherry, and mesquite.

Your handle length should be about 5 to 7" (shorter for smaller tools, longer for larger diameters). For a custom fit, use the width of your palm plus 1" for small tools and the length of your hand from the wrist to the end of middle finger for larger tools.

The handle diameter tapers from about 7/8" to 1-1/8" or so (narrow at the butt end with a slight bulge at the tool end to accommodate the shank). I like my middle finger to nearly touch my palm when wrapped around the smallest diameter of the handle.

For ferrules, 1/2" or 5/8" brass compression nuts or stainless steel tubing work well.

Photos by Frank Miller

AW 20:1, p52

Sharpening your cove tool

Choose any hardened and tempered tool steel rod (3/32" to 1/2" in diameter, 3" to 7" long). See suggestions in the box Steel Options.

With an abrasive chop saw or coarse 36-grit grinding wheel, cut or grind the rod to an angle between 35° and 45°. (Mine are about 40°.)

Hollow-grind the final angle on a medium or fine 8" wheel using either an angled tool rest or a grinding jig. You may need a handle or temporary holder (a dowel with a hole in the end works fine) to get enough length to use an arm-type grinding jig such as the Wolverine jig.

Hone off the grinding burrs by laying the tool on a fine, flat bench stone. Move the tool lengthwise.

Steel options

I use discarded reamers and drill bits, but you must be sure to test the end you plan to sharpen with a file to be sure it is hardened. (If the file skates like glass across the surface, it's hardened. If the file digs in, the steel is soft.)

- The chuck end of most tools is left soft to reduce brittleness and to allow a better grip. If you cut off the flutes, the adjacent portion of the shaft is hardened for a short distance.
- You may find pre-hardened O1, W1, A2, or M2 precision drill blanks or M2 "Dixie pins" (6" lengths) at machinist supply companies such as Enco, Dixie Tool Crib, or MSC.
- Drill rod, on the other hand, is usually annealed and must be hardened and tempered in a heat-treating oven. Members might split the cost to have a batch of blanks heat-treated.
- If you use high-carbon steel, remember when grinding you must not let the temperature get above 250° F, or the hardness will be compromised. The Internet has good information on hardening and tempering carbon steels.

Now, put the tool to use

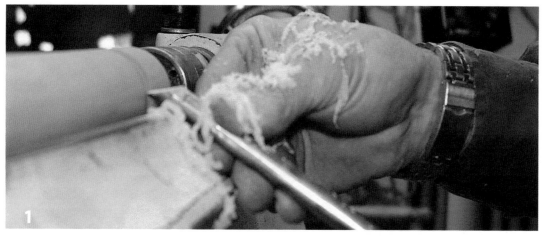

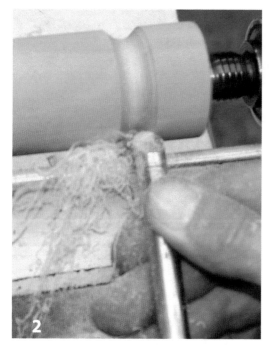

To begin a cove, place the tool on the tool rest perpendicular to the spindle. Keep the the handle low so that the concave "cutting face" is facing up and is almost horizontal. The cutting tip should be at center or slightly above.

To widen and shape the cove, raise the handle a little so the "cutting face" is now tilted slightly downward. Cut downhill on alternate sides of the cove.

To shear scrape the cove to final shape and smoothness, raise the handle until the body of the tool is almost horizontal (the cutting face will be angled down considerably). Cut downhill on alternate sides of the cove. The shear scraping action should produce a fine finish.

Stacey Hager is a member of the Central Texas Woodturners Association of Austin. He has been a frequent contributor to **American Woodturner** *magazine.*

Cove Tool Set

Stacey Hager

For a nice addition to your tool collection, make a graduated set of cove tools with a matching tool caddy. My set includes six cove tools with diameters of 3/32", 1/8", 5/32", 3/16", 1/4" and 5/16". These all fit nicely into a 6-1/2" x 3-5/8" box. You might want to save the box until last to be sure you make it high enough to clear the caddy plus tools and handle.

Tool caddy

The tool caddy has an aluminum center pin the same diameter as the largest tool (see *Figure 1*). Around the perimeter of the caddy I spaced six holes (just a hair larger than the diameter of the largest tool). For the five smaller tools, I made 1-1/2" long aluminum adapters so that all the tools would fit the same handle.

You can turn aluminum on a wood lathe with a gouge or scraper. Use light cuts and be careful of long continuous shavings that can wrap around fingers and cause severe cuts.

Note: Never try to remove metal shavings with the lathe running.

I adjusted the depth of the hole in each adapter so that the overall length of the tools would decrease with the diameter (this makes it easy to keep them in order). Attach the adapters with medium CA glue.

Handle

For the handle, you need a hard, flexible wood that can be threaded to make a collet chuck. Boxwood

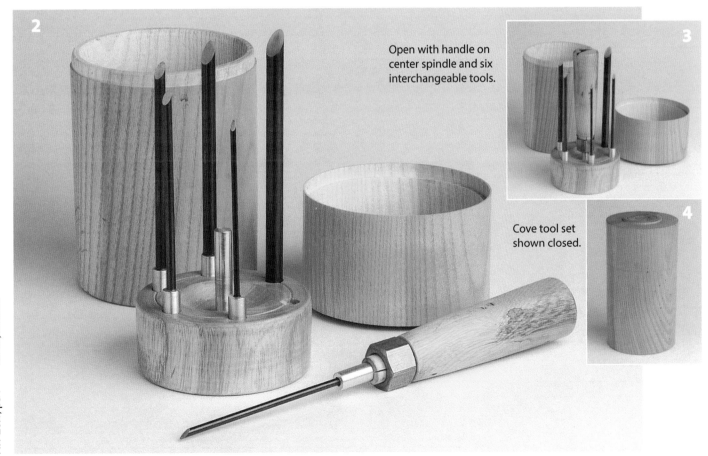

1

is excellent, but almost any wood can be threaded if saturated with CA glue.

The length of the handle should be about 1-1/2" greater than the widest part of your palm. In the end of the handle blank, drill a 1-1/2"

2

3
Open with handle on center spindle and six interchangeable tools.

4
Cove tool set shown closed.

AW 20:1, p54

deep hole the diameter of the largest tool. Use a cone on your live center to align this hole while turning the handle. I use a 20 threads per inch (tpi) hand-thread chaser to thread my handle for a standard 1/2" brass compression fitting (available at most hardware stores).

Note: You may have to use a larger 5/8" x 18 tpi compression fitting if you plan to have your set go all the way to 1/2" diameter. You can also thread your handle with a Bonnie Klein or Willard Baxter threading set-up. A sharp metal-cutting die will work if you repeatedly saturate the threaded area with thin CA glue, but an easier alternative to threading is to use a small drill chuck, but the balance of the tool will not be as nice.

Next, prepare the chuck area. You will need a dial caliper or some device that measures internal and external diameters to the nearest thousandth of an inch.

Measure the internal diameters of the threaded and non-threaded openings of the compression fitting and its length. (My 1/2" fitting measurements: threaded, .635"; non-threaded, .506"; length, .560"). Calculate the thread depth by dividing 0.866 (from a machinist formula for calculating thread depth) by the number of threads per inch (tpi). (Thread depth = .866 /20 tpi = .043".)

The diameter of the wood to be threaded is the internal diameter of the compression fitting threads plus 2 x thread depth. (For 1/2" compression fitting with 20 tpi: internal thread diameter, .635" + 2 x .043" = .721"). Subtract 2 or 3 thousands for clearance and the diameter should be about .719".

The length of the tenon to be threaded is the length of the fitting + about 1/4" (1/8"

clearance front and back). (For a 1/2" compression fitting the length = .560" + .250" or .810". At this point (using a 1/2" compression fitting as the example), you should have a .719" diameter tenon .810" long protruding from your handle with a 1-1/2" deep hole down the center.

With a narrow parting tool, cut a clearance groove 1/8" wide and down to .635" diameter at the base (handle end) of the tenon. Next, cut the front (nose end) of the tenon down to a diameter of .506" or a little less (.500" is ideal) so it will fit through the non-threaded opening in the fitting. This clearance cut also needs to be about 1/8" wide. Taper the resultant step to match the taper on the inside of the fitting. This forms the ramp or incline that will close the collet as the fitting is screwed on as shown in *Figure 5*.

Now, thread the remaining .719" diameter portion of the tenon. Saturate with thin CA glue, allow to

dry, thread a little, re-saturate, then thread a little more until completed. Finally, with a thin dovetail saw, make 2 cuts (90° to each other) from the tip of the collet down all the way to the base. This produces the four threaded fingers, which will close as you tighten the collet. Finally, lubricate the threads with a thin layer of wax.

Use your collet handle for each of the cove tools, as the tool-caddy handle, and for any other tool of similar diameter.

Figures 2, 3 and 4 show one example of a lidded box you can turn for your cove tools.

Stacey Hager is a member of the Central Texas Woodturners Association of Austin. He has been a frequent contributor to American Woodturner *magazine.*

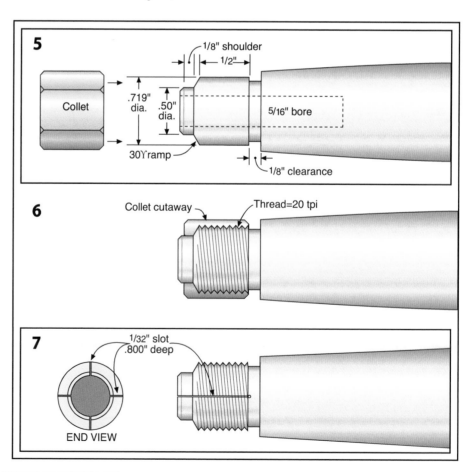

Carbide Cutters

Lyle Jamieson

Photos by David Speckman Photography

AW 26:6, p21

This article will discuss carbide cutters and how to use them for woodturning.

During my lifetime of working with wood, I've acquired information from others—reading books, attending demonstrations, and one-on-one conversations—as well as from personal experience. I had a learning curve to go through with carbide cutters, and this time much of my research came from the Internet, as well as from my own experience. There are conflicting viewpoints expressed on the Internet, but there is consensus enough to support my conclusions.

History

A few years ago, Mike Hunter asked me to consider using carbide cutters on my boring-bar system. In spite of my initial comment, "No thanks, carbide does not get sharp enough for turning," Mike began my education. He described the new technology of nanograin carbide. "Okay," I said, "prove it." And he did—my assumption was wrong.

Carbide cutters have been in use for decades: metal machining, military, sports, plastics, wood-production duplicators, and in flat woodworking for tablesaw-blade tips. The earliest mention I found for carbide was in the 1860s, but the woodturning tool market did not accept carbide until recently.

The first commercially produced use of carbide for turning that I know of was when Dennis Stewart put a carbide tip on his slicer tool, sometime in the early 1990s. It was the precursor of the coring systems used today. While it had wear resistance better than HSS or carbon steel, it would not get as sharp. For the use Dennis intended, however, it was perfect. Then why didn't other uses of carbide take off with Dennis's example? The answer is: *That carbide did not get as sharp as high-speed steel, and a diamond hone was required to sharpen it.*

Metallurgy

There are many different carbides and grades of carbide. Carbide is not just carbide. The quality of the manufacturing varies greatly, and the particles that make up the carbides are different sizes. A microscope is needed to see the difference. Let's break down carbide cutters into two categories. First is *tungsten carbide*. It is formulated from a gray powder and the result is three times stiffer than steel.

The second category is the new *nanograin tungsten carbide*, sometimes referred to as *micro-grain carbide*. The nanograin, as you might guess, is made of much smaller particulate than for tungsten carbide—the difference in grain size is that of BBs to beach balls. Nanograin carbide grains are cemented with another metal, usually cobalt *(Figure 1)*. Generally, there is 6% to 12% binder in the carbide. With optimum grade selection, submicron-grain-size particles of tungsten carbide are manufactured to have a razor edge. What does this have to do with us in the turning world?

Start with a sharp edge

In woodturning, we begin with a sharp edge on our tools, and the instant we start turning, the sharpness of the edge degrades. Let's do some math. Take a 10"-diameter bowl and calculate the circumference: 10 × 3.14 = 30+". Thirty inches of wood are passing the cutter every rotation. Let's say we are turning at 1,000 rpm. In one minute we have just cut 30,000" of wood—almost one-half mile or 500" per second. Will any tool retain its sharp edge very long?

After the initial sharpened edge is gone, the structure of the base material the cutter is made from is left. This remaining cutting edge is called the *land*. With carbide, the base material is very wear resistant and the tool will cut reasonably well for a long time on the land before the edge deteriorates enough to become unusable.

With nanograin carbide, the finer particulate will allow the edge to be even sharper to begin with than with the old carbides—manufacturers are able to produce a razor-sharp edge. The land edge left after the initial nanograin razor-sharp factory edge has been used to cut wood will still be sharp because the fine grain structure is resistant to wear.

How can you tell if your tools are made from the old-style carbide or the new nanograin carbide? The nanograin carbide is manufactured under high heat and high pressure. The surface ends up with a mirror or glossy finish. The old carbide will have a dull, flat-gray appearance. To confuse the distinction, some carbide manufacturers apply coatings to enhance sharpness. These coatings are usually yellow or gold in color and they are intended to mask the dull gray. The coating wears off quickly and the tool is now cutting with the land made of the same base metal structure.

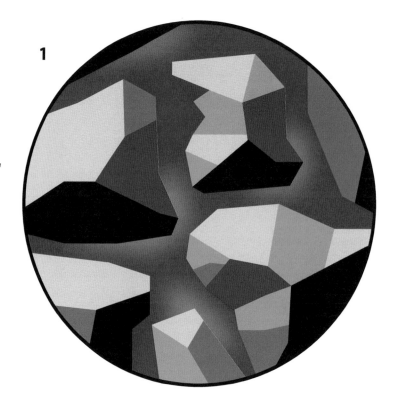

1

Magnification of carbide: Illustration of (gray) carbide cemented with (red) cobalt under high magnification.

Grain sizes and sharpness

I spoke with Tom Walz, President of Carbide Processors Inc. in Tacoma, WA, to compare nanograin carbide to HSS. He said, "Consider that the sharpness level of HSS is in the range of 1 to 20, with 1 being the sharpest possible for HSS starting out. Nanograin carbide, on the other hand, starts out at 2 or 3 sharpness. Turning with both for the same amount of time, HSS is dull and has reached a 20 while nanograin carbide is still sharp at a 4 or 5 in the 1 to 20 range." My conclusion is that the finer structure of nanograin carbide will begin with and hold a sharper edge than the old carbide and stay sharper longer than HSS. This is demonstrated to me in daily use of the Hunter nanograin carbide tools on my boring-bar system.

With HSS tools, the sharpened edge will degrade rapidly, but we can go quickly to the grinder and constantly renew the sharp edge to optimal performance. The sharpened edge of HSS tools will be sharper than the old-style carbide ever gets. You also can use a burr on HSS tools that is not present on carbide. Other steels like stainless and composites have the same trade-off. The knife industry has been struggling with this issue for centuries. The old carbon-steel knives would get sharper and last reasonably well for culinary needs, but they rust and their appearance was a problem. Flat woodworkers have been arguing forever about the best tool steel for router bits and carving tools.

Why use carbide?

Nanograin carbide tools cannot be resharpened to their original razor-sharp factory edge; they are designed to be disposable. They are, however, economical because they last so long. I believe they will wear up to 100 times longer than HSS.

Nanograin carbide cutters leave a much better surface on the wood than the old carbide. Why? Because it begins and remains sharper, and we can use a slicing cut that leaves a cleaner surface on the wood.

How woodturners use carbide tools

There are two types of cuts we can make while turning wood: a scraping cut or a slicing cut. It does not matter whether the tool is HSS or a carbide. The rule for scraping is the cutting edge must touch the wood at a 90° angle or less. Cutting at the centerline with the scraper held flat on the toolrest, the 90° angle is achieved by having the handle slightly up from horizontal (nose of the tool pointing slightly down). As the wood passes by the cutting edge, it scrapes some wood off. If we touch the wood with any sharp edge at more than a 90° angle, handle down with a scraper, the tool will dig in, starting a catch.

The rule for a slicing cut is the bevel behind the cutting edge must be supported against the wood. If you are slicing on an angle without bevel support, the cutting edge will grab, dig in, and skate across the wood's surface until you get a catch. This is a critical concept to understand and when you understand it, tool catches will become a thing of the past (see *Figure 2*).

The two different carbides are used for different cuts for different reasons. The old carbide is used in the scraping mode. Carbide cutters are especially useful for beginners. Learning to use a scraper is easy, and they can scrape for hours and their tool will still be sharp enough.

Old-style carbide cutters are also great for what they were originally made for—roughing out. The turner just presents the tool to the wood in a scraping mode and just pushes it into the spinning wood and scrapes away, keeping the handle slightly up, never violating the 90°-angle rule. The old carbide cutters are wear resistant, so going through dirty bark and miles and miles of waste wood, they will hold their edge for a long time, longer than HSS scrapers. The trade-off is that the old carbide cutters are not as sharp as HSS scrapers or bowl gouges, which is okay—we are using them as roughing tools.

The new nanograin carbide can be used for either a scraping cut or a slicing cut. Professional turner Mike Jackofsky has set up the nanograin cutters to work only in the scraping mode with

2

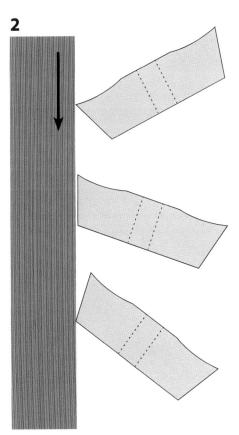

Nanograin carbide cutter in three positions tilted to cut wood (or not).

A

Figure A. Carbide cutter clock positions for a nanograin cutter on ³⁄₁₆" (5 mm) square shaft to be used with swiveling-head boring bar.

Figure B. The carbide cutter is shown cutting under the shoulder of a vessel. The cutting motion can be in both directions, as indicated by the arrow. Notice the swivel has positioned the cutter to allow scraping at the 9:00 position. This means the carbide cutter is cutting at the 9:00 position and is directed toward the tailstock when cutting under the rim of the vessel. Note the obstacle created by leaving the waste wood behind the cutter, which could easily become a problem later.

B

3

The direction of cut is to the left when the carbide-cutter insert is angled to the left. The ring visible in the photo shows the transition shoulder between the surface of the wood just cut and the wood ahead of the cutter. Notice the large thickness of the shaving. The cutting motion is slightly pulling away from the tip, on a taper, across the bottom of this vessel. This hogging-off cut is aggressive and removes large quantities of wood quickly.

4

This bevel-supported cut in the bottom of the vessel is made with the cutter at the 12:00 position, angled to the left, and the direction of the cut is to the left. Note the fine shavings as a light cut is taken.

5

A light cut, riding the bevel, and slicing part way up the side of the hollow form produces a smooth surface. The cutter is cutting at the 12:00 position and the cut is to the left.

6

This is the correct way to undercut a shoulder by removing the waste wood from behind the cutter before working on the underside of the shoulder. The cutter is at the 12:00 position, riding the bevel, and slicing up the side wall to the left.

a tip angle dedicated to scraping across the bottom, inside a hollow form. Mike Hunter developed his new Hercules tool to scrape in this manner, which works better than the old carbide because it is sharper.

Mike Hunter, Trent Bosch, Eliminator, or Jamieson tools have set up the nanograin carbide inserts so the bevel can be used in a slicing action to get a smoother, cleaner surface on the wood. It acts as a hook tool or ring tool to slice through the endgrain fibers of a hollow form or lidded box. Mike Hunter has great tutorials on using nanograin carbide for slicing and scraping in bowls and hollow forms on his website, hunterwoodturningtool.com.

Nanograin carbide: Three cuts possible

The new carbide tool is one complex little workhorse. The 3/16" (5 mm) nanograin carbide cutter is efficient and in this case, smaller is better. Larger cutters stress the wood and the chucking method. Using this small cutter, it is easier to hollow deeper vessels without vibration. The turner takes many smaller cuts quickly rather than slowly grinding away with a larger cutter bit.

If you set it up as I do in my captured boring-bar system, there are three different cuts possible.

Let's envision the cutter assembly locked in a boring-bar swivel assembly and positioned straight forward. Looking toward the headstock and down on the cutter, imagine a clock face *(Figure A)*. When presenting the 8:30 to 9:30 section of the cutter to the wood, the cutting action mimics that of a negative-rake scraper *(Figure B)*. The arrow indicates we can cut in both directions while scraping.

The second type of cut is to use the cutter from the 10:00 to 12:00

section. The result is an angled slicing action that is efficient and easy to cut with (Figure 3). In fact, this is the workhorse section of the cutter that gets most of the use and abuse; wood can be hogged off. There is no bevel support for this cut or for the scraping cut. Note the arrow in *Figure 3*: Only cut to the left.

At the 12:00 position of the cutter, a bevel-supported cut is the result. It is a slicing action and leaves a smooth and clean surface behind. This cut is intended for removing only a small-shaving slice to clean up tool marks and prepare to sand, if needed (*Figure 4*). To make a bevel-supported cut, you must swing the handle to keep the bevel on the surface of the wood to make a curved shape inside a hollow vessel. As indicated by the arrow, the cutting action is to the left.

Even if the entry hole is small, the swivel will allow the 12:00 position to be used in any quadrant of the vessel, bottom, side, or top. This will require working in stages as you move the swivel often to position the cutter to use the bevel at the 12:00 position. The inside contour achieved from this method is really sweet because it is easy to pick up the line from a previous stage and carry it through the next stage (*Figure 5*). With a little practice, the line that the bevel and cutter follow will be superior to scraping cuts. (A laser-measuring device will help monitor the transition from stage to stage and keep a uniform wall thickness.)

The cutter will not cut in the 12:00 to 3:00 position. If you present this quadrant to the wood, it will just rub the shaft and the bottom edge of the cutter, and may even result in some chatter and/or vibration.

One caution to keep in mind: Do not combine the ride-the-bevel and the hogging-off cuts—that combination removes too much

wood, too fast, and starts some vibration going. Doing both cuts simultaneously stresses the chucking method, stresses the wood, and stresses the boring bar. The trick to hogging off fast and easy is to cut with a slight sweeping or scooping motion to pull away from the bevel slightly as you cut. This will create a slight curve to the inside surface of the vessel (see *Figure 3*).

Learning curve

HSS cutters attached to the end of boring bars can be directed left, right, in, or out to produce a cut. With a nanograin carbide cutter, however, there is a bit of a learning curve. For example, the cutting action of the carbide cutter will always be to the left if it is angled or facing to the left. The direction the cutter is facing dictates the direction of the cut. It will try to "climb" if you try to cut in the opposite direction. Going the wrong way will not usually produce a catch, but it will cause the cutter to skate.

When hollowing under a high shoulder, make sure to get the waste wood out of the middle behind the shoulder of the vessel (*Figure 6*). *Figure 2* shows the incorrect way to hollow by leaving the waste wood in the way behind the cut. Removing the waste wood will prevent an inadvertent skate should you bump the wood behind the cut with the back side of the tool.

Figure 4 shows the correct direction for cutting the endgrain on the bottom of a hollow form. *Figure 6* shows the correct direction of a cut coming up the side of a hollow-form vessel. The cutter needs to cut pulling toward the shoulder of the vessel when the cutter is swiveled to the left. And in *Figure 6*, "left" is actually pulling the cut toward the tailstock. *Figure 2* shows the negative-rake scraping cut used to undercut the shoulder area.

The shearing/slicing cut of the nanograin carbide cutter produces a shaving. A scraping cut would produce sawdust. Try one of these little cutters on the nastiest wood you can find and you will be a believer. These nanograin carbide cutters excel in wet wood, dry wood, hard wood, and soft wood. There is no sharpening and they are economical. I find them to be easy and fast for hollowing, and I like it that there is less sanding required. It takes making a few vessels to master the cuts, but it is worth the effort.

Lyle Jamieson is a full-time woodturning sculptor and instructor from Traverse City, MI. Lyle is known for his figurative sculptures and for the Jamieson boring bar and laser measuring system. For more about Lyle, visit his website, lylejamieson.com.

Getting the Most from Scrapers

Richard Raffan

On the first day I turned wood, as I entered his workshop, Douglas Hart said, "You might have heard that real woodturners never use scrapers, but we find them pretty useful." That was 1970, and I hadn't a clue what he was talking about. I forgot his comment until seven years later when I was told by a turner destined to be a renowned pedant, that I had interesting techniques but scrapers should never be required. By then I'd come to regard scrapers as essential for many jobs and had developed a range of scraping techniques using gouges.

I continue to meet novice turners who feel guilty that they even own scrapers, so the myth is perpetuated. It makes me wonder if the perpetuators are limited in their turning activities and abilities, superstitious, or merely ignorant. Whatever the reason, their assertions are of little benefit to the craft.

As a turner of bowls, endgrain boxes, and scoops, I've always found that scrapers enable me to arrive at the shapes I want with maximum speed, efficiency, and above all, with control and minimal sanding. Scraping techniques frequently produce glasslike surfaces right off the tool, especially on the endgrain of tropical hardwoods such as cocobolo or African blackwood. On bowls, scrapers will often improve a gouge-cut surface: The inside of the claret ash bowl in *Figure 1* couldn't be cut much cleaner.

It's certainly true that when turning spindles, scrapers should not be required, but they make life a lot easier when hollowing endgrain—try using a gouge to square the inside of an endgrain box, or turn a flat-bottomed dovetailed rebate for an expanding chuck.

Selecting scrapers

The scrapers I use all the time are shown in *Figure 2*. The scraper I use in a given situation will have a radius only slightly tighter than the curve I'm intending to cut. The scrapers with broad-radius edges (top of *Figure 2*) are primarily for bowls, while the tighter radiuses (bottom of photo) are for hollowing into endgrain.

The square-end and spear-point scrapers (to the right) are for convex curves and getting into corners when hollowing boxes or detailing around beads.

The standard square-section scrapers I use are high-speed steel (HSS) or Kryo steel and mostly ⅜" (9 mm) thick for cuts more than 2" (50 mm) over the toolrest. The narrower tools, 1/2" (13 mm) or less wide, although used very close to the toolrest, are never less than 3/16" (5 mm) thick, with 1/4" (6 mm) thick being preferable.

Heavy scrapers, 1/2" to 3/4" (13 mm to 19 mm) thick, are worth avoiding, however inexpensive. They are tedious to grind and offer

AW 27:2, p20

strength and weight not required on such short tools. A better option for working a long way over the toolrest is a boring bar with a replaceable square cutter, but make sure the cutters are the same width as the bar and are on top of it.

Controlling leverage can be a problem so it pays to have long handles. An old rule-of-thumb says a handle needs to be four times the length of the distance between the toolrest and the cutting point of the edge.

Shaping and grinding

All my scrapers start off with bevels of about 45°, which on rounded edges steepen until vertical on the side. If you're grinding on a 6" (150 mm) wheel, however, an edge can become very fragile, so a double bevel is preferable. Those in *Figure 3* are typical. I don't want a long bevel on the side of a scraper because that makes it too grabby.

Before grinding any scraper, I hone the top. This can be accomplished using a diamond hone, but generally I use the well-worn 180-grit sanding disk stuck between my grinder rests (*Figure 4*).

For decades I've used an edge straight off a 60-grit wheel, only honing the edge for very hard and dense timbers at one end of the spectrum, and very soft woods at the other. For the easy-to-work timbers suited to production work (ash, cherry, teak, yew, and fruitwoods), I've used an edge straight off the wheel and get shavings like the ones in *Figure 1*. But all that might be about to change: A couple of times I've used the new-to-turners cubic boron nitride (CBN) grinder wheels that seem to produce a much finer edge with less chance of burning an edge. They're expensive, but getting my serious consideration.

For scrapers that are near square-ended, you can adjust the platform to

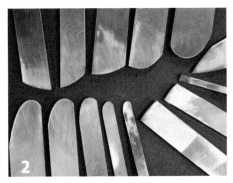

The inside of this ash bowl barely needs sanding after a gentle sweep with a bowl scraper.

Bowl/facework scrapers (top); tools for hollowing endgrain (bottom); square-end and spear-point scrapers for convex curves and getting into corners (to the right).

the desired angle, then keep the tool flat on it as you ease the edge into the wheel (*Figure 5*). The idea then is not to force the edge into the wheel, burning the thin cutting edge. Think in terms of letting the wheel come to the tool with minimal tool pressure against the grinder wheel. With the platform set in position, touching up an edge should take only two or three seconds. On my high-speed grinder I have my platform set for skew chisels, so for all other tools I'm using only the top of the platform to support the tool. I bring the bevel heel onto the wheel, then raise the handle until I see sparks come over the top of the edge. With HSS and Kryo tools, there are few sparks, so when the edge changes color slightly, stop grinding, (*Figure 6*).

To grind a round profile to the cutting edge, I tend to push the tool up the wheel (*Figures 7, 8*) rather than swing the handle sideways, as the edge is less likely to catch or flatten out.

General approach

As a general rule and to avoid catches, scrapers should be used flat on the toolrest—that is, not tilted on edge. After that, make sure the blade tilts down slightly so the angle between the wood and the top of the tool is less than 90°. The currently popular negative-rake scrapers aim to make scrapers more forgiving

and you don't need to be quite so careful about the blade angle, but I'd still aim to keep the edge down, especially on a flat face or in the bottom of a bowl. I see no advantage in a negative-rake grind when all you need to do is raise the handle of any standard scraper to achieve the desired angle between the wood and upper bevel.

Use a straight rather than curved toolrest. On a curved toolrest inside a bowl, a scraper must be kept horizontal or tilted up, which can be dangerous: If you drop the handle, the scraper is supported where the sides contact the toolrest, but the edge points up and is likely to catch. If you raise the handle to drop the edge, then the flat blade rocks on the curve of the toolrest and that also leads to catches. Curved toolrests and scrapers don't go well together.

I have lots of scrapers of various ages, widths, and lengths, and I never use one longer than is necessary. To cut flowing and smooth curves, I choose a tool with an edge that has a radius only slightly tighter than the curve I'm cutting. I find creating a long curve using a narrow round-nose scraper really difficult, no matter how smoothly I move the tool. I also try never to have the tool blade at 90° to the surface I'm cutting. It's usually much easier to have the blade at an angle to the surface you're

The bevels on my scrapers start at about 45° on the nose, becoming near vertical on the side.

The bevels on my scrapers start at about 45° on the nose, becoming near vertical on the side.

The bevels on my scrapers start at about 45° on the nose, becoming near vertical on the side.

cutting so you can drag or push the edge around a curve or across a face of a bowl base.

Used aggressively for rough hollowing bowls or enclosed forms, square-end scrapers can shift a lot of waste in seconds. Using a 1" square-end scraper, it took me about 45 seconds and five cuts to hollow most of the 4" × 8" (10 cm × 20 cm) bowl in *Figure 9*. Provided cuts are

directed nearly parallel to the lathe axis, toward the headstock and within the diameter of the chuck or faceplate securing the job, you can be quite aggressive and force the edge into the wood. Negative-rake scrapers are not so efficient here because the corners are not on top of the tool.

At all other times, and especially when making finishing cuts, you should think in terms of letting the wood come to the tool (rather than pushing the tool into the wood). You need to hold an edge firmly in position so the wood is shaved as it comes onto the edge. And, as the wood is shaved, ease the edge forward. Don't use more than half the edge at a time, and even less as you cut beyond the diameter of the chuck jaws and farther from center.

For finishing cuts, use the same scrapers for delicate stroking cuts. Tool pressure against the wood is about the same as when you rub your hands under a hot-air dryer.

Scrapers on bowls

Figure 10 illustrates a number of ways scrapers can be used for refining surfaces on a bowl. Both the round-nose and V-shaped spear point are more often used tilted on edge to shear scrape. Each of the others has a radius slightly tighter than the curve it's cutting.

Working into corners or around beads, skewed scrapers enable you to get better detail (*Figure 11*). To shear scrape up to a bead or into a corner you need a spear point.

I try never to use scrapers on the upper half of a thin bowl, especially if it's a thin open form, as the wood is inevitably flexible. Catches are almost guaranteed if the scraper is flat on the toolrest. I prefer to cut in from the rim cleanly using a gouge. If, however, scraping techniques are the only way to eliminate chatter marks and

torn grain (other than sanding), never attempt to use a scraper flat on the toolrest near a rim. Instead, shear scrape by tilting your scraper on edge (*Figure 12*). I support the rim as I clean up the inside using an asymmetric round-nose scraper. Dropping the speed a few hundred RPMs makes the task less exciting when things go wrong.

Long before I began shear scraping with scrapers (which for years I wrongly thought too dangerous), I used gouges for similar cuts to great effect, mostly for eliminating small bumps on bowl profiles. The gouge must be rolled right on its side so it doesn't catch (*Figure 13*), and I still prefer this technique for truing up a bowl rim that's running slightly out of whack, or to cut the rim of a face or base in preparation for a shear cut using a scraper.

Hollowing endgrain

The scrapers I use on and into endgrain form the bottom row in *Figure 2*. All my round-nose scrapers are asymmetric with the left wing longer than the right because I always work inboard (to the right of the headstock) so I never need a symmetrically domed scraper. These are ground with a 45° bevel on the nose that becomes ever steeper to the side like the bottom two scrapers shown in *Figure 3*.

These scrapers are not profile cutters: If you get the entire edge in contact with the wood at once, you'll have a big catch. The idea is to use only a small portion of an edge at a time, and by swinging the handle around you can use all of the edge at some time.

I use an edge with a radius only slightly tighter than the curve I'm trying to cut, which makes it easy to develop smooth and flowing curves. When finishing an interior of a hollow like the one in *Figures*

6 **7** **8**

To grind a rounded edge, use the top edge of the toolrest to support the tool and push the tool up the wheel.

9

Using a 1" square-end scraper, it took me about 45 seconds and five cuts to hollow most of the 4" × 8" (10 cm × 20 cm) bowl.

10 **11**

Working into corners or around beads, skewed scrapers enable you to get better detail. Spear-points enable you to shear-scrape right into corners.

12

Never use a scraper flat on the toolrest near a rim. Instead, shear scrape by tilting your scraper on edge.

13

To shear-scrape using a gouge, the tool must be on its side.

14, 15, and *16,* I opt for the larger scraper (to the left in the photos) and avoid using the narrower scraper (to the right). In this situation the tool moves out from the center, and in from the rim, barely brushing the wood to remove little more than dust and tiny curly shavings. If you move the tool smoothly with minimal pressure against the wood, flowing curves should follow. And if you get it right in a couple of passes, be grateful and get sanding. Don't feel you have to stick the tool in the hole again. At the rim of the hollow form, you can have the edge tilted up slightly, but at center it must be tilted down. On a tighter curve, a slightly smaller round-nose is used, but again, I use the largest-profile scraper I can fit in without having the whole edge in contact with the wood at once.

My square-end scrapers are actually slightly skewed to the right for getting into corners of a flat-bottomed box (*Figure 17*). This enables me to get into the corner without the right corner of the tool messing up the flat endgrain. The slightly curved edge of a "square end" means you can turn a flat surface without having both corners of the edge in the wood at once.

Enclosed forms

When hollowing enclosed forms I use standard scrapers if the opening is large enough to accommodate them (*Figures 18, 19*). The main irritation in using these tools in this situation is that the large shavings are not easily extracted with the lathe running. Initial roughing is with square-end scrapers (see *Figure 9*), then I complete the inside curves with a round-nose that is as large as can reach the area I'm completing. The more the rim is undercut, the narrower the tool you need.

When there are smaller openings or undercut rims that

Use as large a tool as possible (left) with a radius slightly tighter than the curve you want to cut.

My square-end scrapers are actually slightly skewed to the right for getting into corners of flat-bottomed boxes. The profile of the round-nose scraper is such that the entire cutting edge does not make contact with the wood all at the same time.

I can't reach with a straight blade, I resort to the undercutting tools, which still produce a decent shaving and remove waste in a hurry (*Figure 20*).

If you've been taught that scraping is not something real turners do, I'd urge you to give it a go.

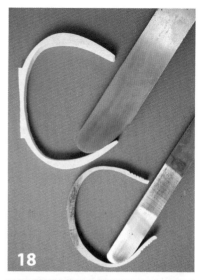

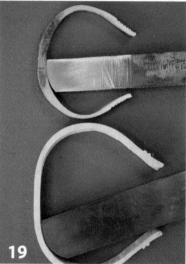

Standard straight blades can be used through quite small openings.

Kelton Undercutters and similar tools let you reach where straight blades cannot.

Richard Raffan is a semi-retired professional turner living in Canberra, Australia. Well known as an author of classic woodturning books and videos, he travels internationally to teach. Visit his website at richardraffan.com.

Heat-Treating Scrapers

John Lucas

When I first started turning wood, I built a lathe using a drill for the drive and a lag screw stuck through a 2x4 as my tailstock. I didn't even know shear cutting tools existed; I made all of my tools from old screwdrivers. These worked OK, but I needed something bigger. An older woodworker suggested files, and so I ground an edge on an old file and went to work. My tool didn't even have a handle, and, though I didn't know then, it was probably too brittle to be used safely.

After years of turning, I occasionally make special tools from an old screwdriver or a file. But, my methods have improved considerably—I've learned how to properly heat treat those metals to prevent injury and to improve their edge holding abilities.

Let me make two things really clear. First, it is dangerous to use a file straight off the shelf without some sort of tempering or softening. Files are extremely hard and therefore brittle. When they shatter, a piece could easily hit your face with extreme force. Second, good quality, commercially made tools will always be better than homemade, unless you have years of experience in heat treating metals and other aspects of metallurgy.

So why make your own tools? It's fun. You get a feeling of pride and accomplishment that I think the old time toolmakers must have experienced. You also learn about metal and heat treating which can help you in all your woodworking; you'll certainly have a better understanding of why high-speed grinders come with warnings that

Figure 1. The author's arsenal of home-made tools, all made from salvaged or readily available materials: above, from left—miniature bowl gouge from a press pin, scrapers from screwdrivers and allen wrenches and parting tool made from a keyhole saw.

Figure 2. Flat skew from a file, a round skew from drill rod and a hollowing bit made from a file. Photos by author.

overheating a tool will remove its temper. And, the process gives you an economical way to experiment with different grinds and cutting angles on your tools.

Now that that's out of the way. I will discuss heat treating in general, then show you how to heat-treat a tool in the simplest way I found — using your barbecue grill and the kitchen oven. Who says men never use an oven for anything?

The simplest tool to make is a scraper or skew from an old file. I look for nice thick files at the flea market. I haven't paid more than a dollar for one yet. As I said, files are too hard and brittle to use as turning

tools, but the tempering process I'll discuss reduces the degree of hardness, making the metal much more useful for our purposes.

The heat-treating process can be divided into three main stages: Annealing, which softens the tool so it can be shaped; hardening which again makes the tool so hard that its cutting edge would be very sharp, but also very fragile; and tempering which helps you reach a compromise between sharpness and toughness.

A well-tempered tool will be hard enough to take a good edge, but soft enough to resist chipping and shattering. The level of tempering must be suited for the

AW 16:1, p14

Figure 3. An ordinary charcoal grill is used for both softening and hardening the metal The metal can be softened, a process called annealing by heating it in the grill, then letting it cool overnight.

Figure 4. To harden the metal it is heated to cherry read, using plenty of fuel, fanned by air forced in from a high dryer or other source, then plunging it into peanut oil, which you can buy in most grocery stores. Hold the metal and swirl it around in the oil to promote even cooling. Work outside, and have fire extinguisher handy, in case the oil catches fire.

tool: a surgeon's scalpel must be incredibly sharp, for example, but it doesn't have to be as tough as an ax.

Annealing metal

The first step is to anneal the file, which softens the metal so it can be shaped and bent without breaking. Blacksmiths do this in a forge, heating the tool to cherry red, then plunging it into dry sand and leaving it there, so that it cools slowly. Blacksmiths often worked in the shade, so they could judge colors more accurately. When ferrous metals like steel become cherry red, they lose the ability to attract a magnet; some workers like to check the temperature this way, as well.

After the metal is annealed, it is soft enough to be shaped and ground to the profile you desire, either with another file or some type of grinder.

Hardening and tempering

The shaped metal will still be too soft to hold an edge and must be hardened before it will make a good tool. Do this by heating the steel to its critical temperature (cherry red or non-magnetic) and then quenching it in oil or water to cool it rapidly. This will make the metal very hard and again it will be too brittle to use.

Tempering is the next step. The tool is reheated, but this time you don't want the metal to become cherry red. The goal for the metal we are using here is to heat it until it is the color of straw and quench it again. Tempering removes some of the brittleness and makes it easier to sharpen but leaves it hard enough to hold an edge. This process takes a skilled blacksmith to get the temperature just right; it's difficult to judge the color and easy to let the piece get too hot, especially if the edge is thin.

At first I used a propane torch and then a hotter Mapp gas torch to heat the file. This worked on small pieces, but I had difficulty heating large pieces evenly. Then I read an article by toolmaker Ron

Hock, recommending using an oven to temper the steel. Then a knifemaker friend recommended using a barbecue grill to anneal the steel. Now I had a simple process that anyone could handle.

My simple process

Here is how my method goes. Start up the charcoal grill and bury the file in the coals. When the coals get red-hot, the file should be also. Ideally the metal should be non-magnetic, but I find this hard to achieve over more than a few inches. The file won't be soft enough for serious work, but will work for what we are doing. The metal must cool slowly, so just let the coals and the file cool down overnight. It is now soft enough to work with common tools. Check it by removing some of the teeth with a good file. I use a grinder to shape the metal and a belt sander set on its back to grind the teeth off the old file. Grind and file the tool into the shape you want.

Now it's time to harden the tool. Fire up the old grill again. Bury the tool in the coals and heat it until it is cherry red and non-magnetic. If you have trouble getting it this hot, blow on the coals with a hair dryer or other small concentrated fan. You've seen old blacksmiths do this with a bellows. Sometimes it can be difficult with thick metal. Pile on plenty of charcoal and try to get the air under the coals. When it reaches the proper temperature, leave it there for 30 minutes per 1/4-in. of thickness. This ensures that the tool will be more evenly hardened. When the time is up (or you run out of patience), grab the metal with a pair of tongs or pliers and plunge it into a bucket of peanut oil. Keep the tool moving in the oil, so it is cooled quickly and evenly. Used motor oil will work, but there is a very real hazard of fire and disposal of the used oil is a problem. Peanut oil is cheap and has a higher flash point. Work outdoors and keep a steel lid handy to put out the fire if it happens. I've done this about a dozen times and have not had a fire, but the potential is there. It is also wise to keep a fire extinguisher handy.

Now the steel is very hard and brittle. To temper the tool, use an oven. The tool should be heated to 375 degrees Fahrenheit. More heat makes the tool softer and less heat makes it harder. Your oven is probably not accurate. Mine was off 50 degrees. Buy an oven thermometer and let the oven stabilize at 375 for 30 minutes or so. Place the tool in the oven on a brick. This helps heat the tool more evenly. Heat the tool for 30 minutes per 1/4-in. of thickness. When it is done plunge it into the oil to stop it from changing. Using my thermometer and oven the tool changes to straw color around 390 degrees so that's the temperature I use.

The tool is now ready to sharpen. I wanted the tang area to be softer for strength, so I wrapped

5

The metal can be tempered, a process which balances its edge-holding ability with toughness, in a home-kitchen oven.

the blade with wet towels and heated the tang with a propane torch until it turned blue. You could heat it red hot and let it cool slowly which would really make it soft, but it's harder to keep the blade at the proper temperature.

That's all there is to it. If you want a tool in a hurry just heat the file to 375 degrees and quench it. It will now be soft enough to use safely. It's a little harder to grind off the teeth and it may not bend without breaking but it won't shatter dangerously. If you want to run a test put the file in a vise and bend it about 90 degrees. A properly annealed tool will bend a pretty good ways before breaking and won't shatter. Do this test with a scrap file. You can still use the broken file to make cutters for hollowing tools. Obviously you should have on all the proper safety gear before trying this.

Using drill rod for tools

I use polished drill rod to make my small hollowing tools and small round skews. Drill rod is fairly hard when you buy it and will cut fairly well without hardening. It is very simple to harden the cutting edge with a propane torch.

I buy AISI-W-1 drill rod. This is a water-hardening metal. That means that water is the correct quenching

medium for this metal. You can get a chart from your dealer showing the heat treating temperatures if you really want to know. I use a small propane torch and heat the tip to cherry red, then quench it in water. Polish the steel so you can watch the color and slowly heat it until you reach a slight straw color then quench it again.

This only hardens the first 1/2-in. or so but on small tools this will last through quite a few sharpenings. When the tool seems to dull quickly just pull out the torch and reharden the tip. It will only take a minute or so to reharden and you'll have a good usable tool again.

There are obviously more precise ways to heat-treat a tool and the quenching medium you choose will cause a lot of argument among blade smiths. This method is based on the safest and easiest way to heat treat an unknown steel by someone who is not a blacksmith. If you are going to make very many tools a forge or oxy-acetylene torch would obviously be easier.

Hope you have as much fun making tools as I have.

John Lucas is a professional photographer who has been working with wood for 35 years, and turning wood for 25. He is a frequent demonstrator at turning events.

Negative Rake Scrapers

Stuart Batty

Scraping with a negative angle on a blade is not a new technique. It was originally developed centuries ago for turning ivory and blackwood. However, my technique is slightly different: A burr does the cutting. See what this tool and grind can do for your woodturning.

For those of you who do not know, I am a time-served, apprenticed spindle turner and trained in the art of cutting wood. I served my apprenticeship under my father, Allan Batty (I am sure you all remember him. He is the old one).

When I spindle turn, I do not scrape. However, when I started making more artistic pieces, it became necessary to use some scraping techniques simply because a gouge cannot cut in restricted areas. A prime example is cutting deep in a narrow bowl or inside an end-grain box.

The usual technique of scraping is to grind a shape suitable for the form you intend to cut. The dry grinding wheel creates a burr at the front top edge of the tool, pushing some of the excess metal over the cutting edge. This burr is what does the cutting. However, because a traditional scraper does not have a negative-rake angle, it is often far too aggressive and almost impossible to use on dense exotics—especially on end grain.

In the past, I would hone off the burr, leaving a smooth surface at the top of the scraper. This would make the tool less aggressive. By using a long tool handle, I would have enough control to ensure the tool did not get a catch on the end grain. But, this technique has some limitations.

Deflection problems

If the piece is not extremely secure in the chuck, dense woods will pull themselves onto the scraper and rip out of the chuck. When the wood is thin (example: cutting end grain inside a bowl) and you turn with a traditional scraper with or without the burr, the wood will try to climb onto the edge of the scraper. A burr only compounds the problem.

Deflection is like a clock pendulum: As the wood deflects from the very small grab on the cutting edge, it will bounce away

Cocobolo and Western Australian sheoak thin-walled bowls, 10"x5". Thickness of less than 1/8" was achieved by using the negative-rake scraper on the inside walls.

Photos: Don Dafoe

AW 21:1, p24

and then travel back at the cutting edge the same distance it deflected. This means the wood will now climb even further onto the cutting edge and cause a slightly larger grab on the cutting edge. While the piece is turning at 30 to 60 mph, rapid wood deflection accelerates. Each deflection will be around 1/8" to 1/4" apart, which means the wood will have grabbed and deflected some 24 to 48 times in 6" of rotation. This all occurs in less than one-tenth of a second—far too fast to pull the tool out. The biggest catch is the last one that caused the wood to fail.

BANG! There goes the thin-walled bowl. If you pick up the pieces from the floor, examine the increased catches. You will see a

Western Australian sheoak; 10 × 5". Stuart used a negative-rake scraper on only the inside walls. The wall thickness of each piece is 7/64".

series of progressively deeper and deeper catches in the end grain.

A different problem

As the tool starts to cut the wood, which does not flex, it will pull the thin blade into the end grain, causing a small catch. This will cause the blade to deflect (slight bend); it will then rebound back into the wood but even deeper, causing a larger deflection and rebound. This happens many times in a fraction of a second—far too fast for you to react in time before the big catch, which will pull a very large chunk out of the wood and kick the tool away from the work. This will give you a big fright and make you very nervous about putting the tool to the surface. Therefore, you will hold the tool more firmly and when you put it to the wood surface again, it will just catch the tool even harder.

This is the time to try negative-rake scraping.

Negative-rake solution

I have been making square bowls since 1982; this is a style I pioneered, which stems from being a spindle turner. As a spindle turner, I cut a lot of pommels for both balusters and newel posts. (A pommel is the square shoulder cut at either end of the baluster or newel post.) Therefore, when I started turning square bowls, I found it easy to cut through the square corners or any broken surface, including natural edges.

Until recently, I always cut the corners of all the types of square bowls with a bowl gouge because the technique is very similar to cutting a pommel. I turned over 250 species of wood in a square bowl format before my spindle-turning technique ran into a wall and would not produce an acceptable finish. Not even my dad could solve this one!

A narrow blade like on this negative-rake scraper is ideally suited to turn tall, narrow exotic bowls. The negatve-rake angle is first ground on the 10V steel so the tool can be touched up many times with a new burr before requiring you to grind the negative angle again.

No matter how I sharpened my gouge, the turned surface of Australian goldfield burls was always torn or chipped. Indeed, the damage to the surface was too deep to sand out. My wall thickness was approximately 1/8" (3mm), and the damage was up to 1/16" on both surfaces of the square bowl.

I knew that goldfield burls are some of the densest burls in the world, with specific gravities from 1.1 to 1.3. These members of the eucalyptus family grow in an arid region of Western Australia. They are one of the few woods that do not cut cleanly with any gouge cut—the surface always chips out.

I had over 20 types of these eucalyptuses to turn and was unable to get a good end result. I knew that it was not possible to scrape it with a regular scraper for two reasons—they were too dense,

The challenges of ivory and blackwood

Ivory has a grain like a dense exotic and will grab on any type of scraper that does not have a negative angle. However, because of its extreme density and 1.84 specific gravity (50 percent greater than any wood known to man), you can turn it with a negative-rake scraper without a burr.

Before mass production, ivory billiard and snooker balls were turned on the lathe. To get extreme accuracy, scraping was essential, and a negative angle on the scraper was required to avoid the ivory grabbing at the tool.

Blackwood is one of the densest woods, with a 1.2 specific gravity (20 percent heavier than water). It is one of the best woods for woodwind instruments due to its harmonics and resistance to absorbing moisture from the breath of the instrument player.

Blackwood is used for the majority of high-quality bagpipes. One essential part of the bagpipe is the chanter; this is the section of the instrument that controls the sound. The chanter is approximately 15" long and tapered along its length—it has a wall thickness of less than 1/8" (3mm) along its full length. This piece of the instrument is by far the hardest part to turn and requires scraping to achieve the accuracy in wall thickness on the outside. The inside is drilled and reamed with a modified World War I French bayonet, which has a three-edge long blade ideal for this purpose.

It is almost impossible to scrape blackwood with a regular scraper blade either with or without the burr. Using a regular blade will cause the wood to grab at the tool and shatter the chanter. Instead, a negative angle is required for the blade to prevent any grabbing.

Due to blackwood's high density, it is not always essential to have a burr. Because the outside is all side-grain turning, the negative-angle tool without a burr will peel off wood fibers.

Off-Center Square Bowl, Western Australian sheoak; 14 × 5 × 3-1/2". "I used negative-rake scraping for the finish cuts on the wing sections of the piece."

and the surface I was cutting was a natural edge. This combination would make a regular scraper grab and add to the fact that the surface I was cutting was only 1/8" thick.

It was at this point that I considered the density of the wood and the fact that the surface was an intermittent cut and only 1/8" thick. I decided to try the old ivory technique of grinding a negative angle (see The Challenges of Ivory). However, after the briefest cut, the tool required a lot of pressure to remove any more wood, and at 1/8" thick, it flexed too much.

As I resharpened the tool and left the burr on it, I found out that the finish was exceptional. The tool I was using was a 3/8" beading and parting tool. However, I was using an M2 steel that had an extremely short life—the burr would only stay on the tool approximately 15 seconds. Since I have the luxury of a lot of tools from teaching spindle classes, I applied the burr to all of them; this way I reduced my trips to the grinder. As one tool dulled, I would simply put it down and pick up the next, which allowed me to focus

on the surface and concentrate on the cut.

Because maintaining a burr is critical, I no longer use M2 steel due to its short cutting life. I've switched to 10V (also known as A-11) because it has the ability to maintain the burr four or five times longer for this cutting. This is a 10 percent vanadium steel, more wear resistant than any cobalt steel. (Vanadium is the most wear-resistant alloy that can be added to steel, including tungsten.)

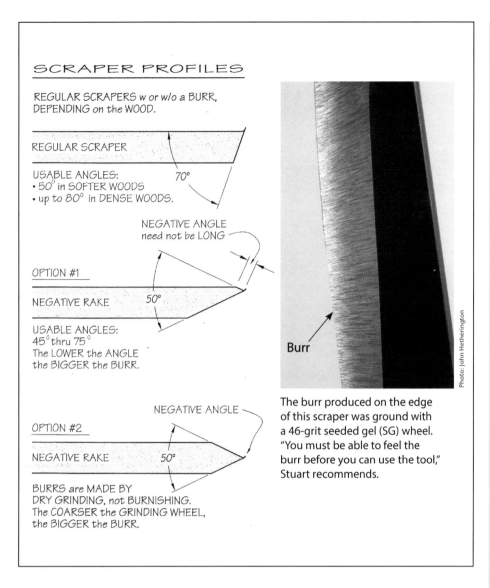

SCRAPER PROFILES

REGULAR SCRAPERS w or w/o a BURR, DEPENDING on the WOOD.

REGULAR SCRAPER

70°

USABLE ANGLES:
• 50° in SOFTER WOODS
• up to 80° in DENSE WOODS.

NEGATIVE ANGLE
need not be LONG

OPTION #1

NEGATIVE RAKE   50°

USABLE ANGLES:
45° thru 75°
The LOWER the ANGLE
the BIGGER the BURR.

NEGATIVE ANGLE

OPTION #2

NEGATIVE RAKE   50°

BURRS are MADE BY
DRY GRINDING, not BURNISHING.
The COARSER the GRINDING WHEEL,
the BIGGER the BURR.

Burr

Photo: John Hetherington

The burr produced on the edge of this scraper was ground with a 46-grit seeded gel (SG) wheel. "You must be able to feel the burr before you can use the tool," Stuart recommends.

Working with these ornery goldfield burls opened my eyes to other opportunities. Now, I grab my negative-rake scraper for all my thin-walled cocobolo bowls and goblets. I also find it ideal for dense exotic woods and oak, yew, cherry, and ash.

Here are a few turning tasks that I've found ideally suited for negative-rake scraping:

- finishing the end grain on the inside of a bowl or goblet
- finishing the end grain on the inside of a box
- finishing the outside of a bowl with side and end grain
- turning where space is restricted
- turning square bowls

Try this technique with a negative angle on top of your scraper. Just remember the burr has a very short cutting life. If you can't feel the burr on top of the edge, it is time to grind the tool again.

As long as you don't point this tool uphill, you'll find this a user-friendly grind.

Stuart Batty (Stuart@woodturning.org), a popular demonstrator, is a third-generation English woodturner who now lives in Colorado. His company, SB Tools, manufactures and sells a line of negative-rake scrapers.

Why the burr is so important

Negative-rake scraping as I define it relies on one essential element: the burr. When scraping ivory and blackwood, the burr is not necessary, mainly due to the densities and structure.

When the blade is ground on the top at an angle and then ground from beneath to produce a burr on the upward edge, the burr does all the work. This is an excellent way to refine shape and remove small tool marks.

This is an easy technique to learn and a great way to get accurate shapes or thickness. Unlike a traditional scraper with a burr, negative-rake scraping is not an aggressive cut—even on dense end grain. However, this is not a bulk-removing technique, as the cutting life of the tool edge is short.

It is essential that there is a burr present on the cutting edge. Once the burr has been worn off, the scraper will not work well and will usually start tearing the grain. This is because you have to apply too much pressure to keep it cutting.

Negative-rake scraping does not require the handle to be higher than the blade like regular scraping or tilted/trailing like shear scraping. However, do not drop the handle too low or it will catch.

Negative-rake scraping is most suited for medium to extremely dense woods. It is not suited for spalted or soft woods. For example: It does not work well on redwood or some types of spalted maple. You can achieve better results for these woods by using a regular scraper with a burr.

Make a Plug-and-Inlay Tool

John Lucas

I have been adding wooden plugs and inlays to my turnings for a long time—cut a hole or groove, turn a plug or ring, glue them in place, then finish-turn everything. Plugs and inlays add a nice touch to many turning projects. To accomplish the mating of the plug and hole or the ring and groove accurately, however, requires precise measurements. If a dimension is just a few thousandths off, I have to either start over or fill the gap with colored epoxy.

One day, while inserting a Morse taper into the tailstock, I thought of a solution to the problem: make a taper on the wooden plug or inlay that fits a matching taper on the hole or groove!

The advantage of this method is that you can sneak up on a perfect fit. All you need is the right tool, a little patience, a hacksaw, and a file. The tool is a scraper with two custom-ground 5° angles.

The clock measures 8" (20 cm) in diameter and is made from mahogany. The plug in the middle is made from laminated wood to achieve a solid-wood look.

Angle jig and tool

Make a jig to use for checking the angle at which to grind the cutting edges of the scraper *(Figure 1)*. The jig does not have to be exactly 5°—all you need is something close. Take a thin piece of metal and color it with a chemical dye or simply use a marker. Scribe a line across it at 90° to the edge. Measure the width you want on the front of your scraper and scribe a line at a 5° angle. Then use a hacksaw and a file to get the shape you want.

Cut a hole for a plug and a recess for an inlay ring.

Glue in the plug and inlay.

The body of the mirror is segmented, as well as the plug and inlay ring.

AW 25:4, p27

Use a jig to aid in creating a 5°-angled scraping tool, which will be used for cutting matching holes and plugs or matching grooves and inlay rings.

Use the jig to mark lines on the scraper tool. Then grind the scraper close to that shape. Undercut the sides and square tip, just like you would when sharpening a scraper. Use the jig to check the shape and angle. Grind slowly to sneak up on a perfect fit. A strip sander makes this easier but a grinding wheel works, too. Then flip the jig over and grind the other side of the tool. This ensures that both sides will be the same angle.

Hone the tool with a diamond hone so it has a burr just like a scraper. It takes time to make the tool but it won't have to be reground for a long time, just occasionally touch up the cutting edge with a hone.

Use of the tool

Cut a hole in the wood for the plug, using a parting tool. Then use the custom scraper tool to fine-tune the edge of the hole to a 5° angle *(Figure 2)*. Do this by holding the scraper at 90° on the toolrest and using the left side of the tool.

Next, turn a plug for the hole from contrasting wood. Measure the hole with calipers and transfer that dimension to the plug blank. Make a mark. Cut up to the mark carefully using a gouge, getting the plug close to the correct size. Then use the 5° scraper to cut the angle on the side *(Figure 3)*. Use the right side of the tool for this cut

and hold the tool at a 90° angle on the toolrest. Sneak up on the size. Check the fit often. At first the plug will just barely fit in the opening of the hole. Each time you remove some wood, the plug will fit deeper into the hole. Stop before the plug bottoms out.

If, however, you want the plug to bottom out for a stronger glue joint, measure the total thickness of the plug and the depth of the hole. Subtract that total from the total thickness of your base piece, and that is how far the plug should stick up. Each time you make a small cut on the plug it will sit deeper into the hole. Stop when you reach the measurement you arrived at earlier. When done correctly, the glue joint will be all but invisible.

Inlay rings

This tool also works when cutting grooves for inlaying rings and the rings themselves, but you have to take much more care when sneaking up on the cuts—both sides of the groove *and* of the ring need to match.

Grain alignment

If you use solid wood for the ring and for the object, make sure the grain aligns to compensate for wood movement so that future glue-joint problems are avoided. Wood movement can also cause problems if you put a segmented ring into a solid piece of wood. The same is true with a solid ring in a segmented piece. Match up solid wood with solid wood or segmented with segmented, and pay attention to grain alignment.

Sometimes, however, I want a solid-wood look for a plug in a segmented object, such as the clock shown here. In that case, I stack-laminate thin pieces of wood with the grain running in different directions like plywood.

Use the left side of the scraper, holding it at 90° on the toolrest, to finish cut the hole for the plug.

Use the right side of the scraper to cut the outside angle of the plug to match the hole cut in the body of the turned object. Hold the tool at 90° on the toolrest.

One last tip: These rings and plugs fit so well that pressure from the glue can force the ring back out or even break the ring while applying clamps. Been there, done that. Simply cut a second groove inside of the original groove (place it in the middle) for the excess glue to flow into. This relieves the pressure to let the inlay ring sit flat.

John Lucas is a professional photographer who has been working with wood for 35 years, and turning wood for 25. He is a frequent demonstrator at turning events.

Making Micro Tools

Wayne Fitch

Some of my friends have accused me of making life harder than it has to be. So when I took up small-scale vessels in the last year, they weren't surprised that I tackled making my own miniature tools, too.

Turning small scale is a rewarding form of turning, and I've found that the techniques carry over to larger turnings. In my opinion, the challenge of turning small emphasizes attention to details. I usually avoid a "miniature" label that would go into a doll house, although numerous people collect this size of turning.

Anyone who has turned small-scale objects has placed a lot of thought with the tools that are available—and more precisely, that aren't available. Returning to my premise that I make life more challenging, I began creating my own tools.

I gathered design opinions from friends who primarily turn miniature-size vessels. From these ideas and the time-tested machinist cutter shapes, I have designed my own set of small-scale tools. Here's what I've learned about making small-scale turning tools.

Although not necessary, it's helpful to drill and turn these tools at a metal lathe. I traded for an EMCO Compact 5 small precision lathe (retail cost: about $1,200). There are several less-expensive brands of small metal lathes on the market.

Begin with the handle

I first realized that a common handle would be more convenient than a separate one for each tool. I decided that the handle should be hollow so each tool shaft could be adjusted for length as needed when cutting and shaping wood.

With that as a starting point, I considered different materials. I found a material called drawn over mandrel (DOM) or what non-metal people call steel tubing. This type of tubing already has an accurate hole through the center and is available in various inside dimensions (ID) and outside dimensions (OD). The DOM that I selected is a 1/2" OD x .120W steel tube available at a local supplier of metals catering to the machinist or www.MetalMart.com.

This size leaves just a few one thousands ID over the 1/4" needed for the tool shafts to slip in—an ideal match.

I decided on 1/4" tool shafts, as this size would be the largest I planned for my turnings. I then studied turning supply catalogs for something comfortable to cover the handle. I settled on a clear vinyl hose that is reinforced with nylon cord. This is available in various

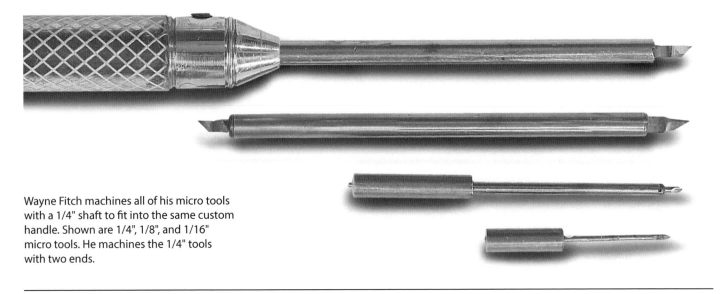

Wayne Fitch machines all of his micro tools with a 1/4" shaft to fit into the same custom handle. Shown are 1/4", 1/8", and 1/16" micro tools. He machines the 1/4" tools with two ends.

AW 18:4, p12

A full-sized gallery of Wayne's hollow vessels from lower left: maple burl and ebony, blackwood, curly koa, unknown Asian wood, and maple burl and blackwood.

ID and OD diameters at home improvement stores.

To build the handle, cut 3/4"-diameter solid brass rod at least 1-1/4" inch long and center bore a 1/4" hole. This fitting at the front of the tool will receive the 1/4" rod for the cutter. After boring the 1/4" hole, I reverse it in the chuck and face the end of the brass to give it an even cut, then center bore a 1/2" hole approximately 1/4" deep. This will be the end that will be epoxied and press-fit on the DOM tube. At this step, you may add decorative turning to the front end of the brass rod.

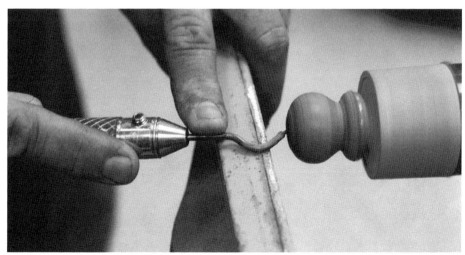

Wayne undercuts the inside of a 1"-diameter hollow form with 1/8" curved tool.

For the butt end of the handle, begin with a brass piece approximately 1-1/4" long. On one end, center drill a 1/2" hole approximately 1/4" deep. You can turn decoration at the opposite end. The length of the handle is personal preference; I usually ask a supplier to cut the DOM tubing in 6" lengths. After I glue and press one end on the DOM tube, I push the vinyl hose over the tubing. You'll need a straight cut on the end of the hose for a square fit up against the brass end. The fit is tight on this tubing; with a little effort the brass piece slides on. Next, cut the vinyl hose 1/4" short for the fitting of the other end of the brass end, which also is pressed and glued.

For the final handle step, drill and tap with a 1/4" x 20 tpi set screw on the end that receives the tool rod. The 1/4" rod will probably hit an obstruction because of burrs from drilling and tapping the set screw hole, so remove the burrs with a round file. I recommend using a bottoming tap (one with a flat end); this creates a better set of threads through the brass. For appearance, polish and lacquer the brass.

Now, make the rods

I next turn my attention to the rods that hold the cutters. After several trials, I settled on 1/4" drill rod (36" length). One mail-order source for this rod is Reid Tool Supply (www.reidtool.com). This drill rod is a good quality low-carbon content steel available in a variety of sizes and types, depending on which hardening method you intend to use.

The rods I have found are:
• O-1, which is an oil-hardening type. This is the rod I rely on because it's machinable when purchased and it is designed to be heat-treated in oil after final machining.

• W-1, which is a water-hardening type. It's hardened in water after machining. Because I've had good results with O-1, I haven't tried the W-1 rod.
• A-1, which is an air-hardening type. Ambient temperature of the air hardens the rod after heating and machining. This type is more difficult to machine before hardening, but bears your consideration.

To accomplish the hardening of O-1 rod, bring up the temperature of the piece with an acetylene-oxygen torch (mapp gas also would work) to a cherry red color, then quench the hot piece in peanut oil purchased from a grocery store. This oil has a high flash point and can tolerate high temperatures. I haven't had any surprise fires but I leave nothing to chance.

All machining must be done before hardening. For straight cutters, I center-drill 3/8" holes in each end. I usually make a double-ended rod to save material, (the other end slides out of the way into the handle). To drill a straight hole for the cutter, you'll first need to face the end of the rod square. I've found 1/4" rod fairly easy to drill straight, but starting the hole with a machinist center drill produces a nicer hole.

Before gluing the cutters, heat the drill rod in peanut oil for 60 minutes in a 400-degree F oven. After an hour, I cool the rods at ambient (room) temperature. This step accomplishes two important things. First, it brings the hardness down slightly, which is referred to as annealing. Secondly, the annealing gives my wife something to talk about as the peanut oil has an odor when heated. After I explain the multi-uses of a kitchen oven, the domestic situation improves.

For an undercutting tool, I drill and bend the rod to the desired

shape when heat-treating. I use either medium or thick viscosity cyanoacrylate (CA) glue to hold the cutting tips. When I need to change a tip, I apply heat to the cutter and it pulls out easily.

Have fun making cutting tips. I've found the choice of cutting tips can be either inexpensive or expensive. HSS cutter stock is inexpensive and is readily available in the round and square stock I prefer.

When you drill the hole in the end of the rods, the 1/8" round HSS cutter will require a 1/8" hole and the square cutter will take a larger hole to allow for the square corners. When drilling, the hole is slightly larger due to a small amount of play as you drill the rod. Using the square HSS cutter creates a larger cavity for the CA glue to bond with.

Carbide is a more expensive choice for the cutters. The expense of carbide is a little more, but the expense really ramps up when grinding to shape and sharpening. Carbide requires a diamond wheel to

Wayne trues up 1-1/2" diameter burl with a micro tool ground similar to a 1/2" round nose scraper.

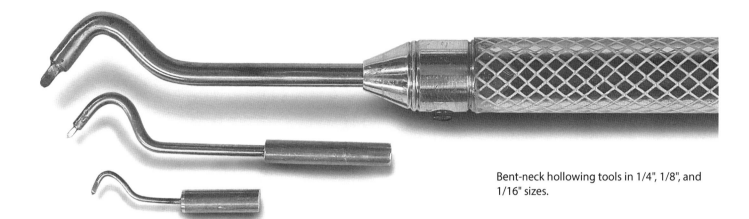

Bent-neck hollowing tools in 1/4", 1/8", and 1/16" sizes.

cut; you can't use the same ordinary grinding wheel to sharpen HSS to shape or sharpen carbide. Carbide requires the expertise and expense of a machine shop with the proper tool grinders. Another carbide drawback is that it's brittle; if you drop the tool on a hard surface, it may shatter. However, if you have a friendly machine shop or access to a diamond wheel, carbide cutters reduce trips to the grinder.

I made a few carbide cutters for special occasions and to continue my quest of complexity. I have had carbide ground in 1/8" inches and in 1/4" for cutters in larger tools. Yes, carbide does cut better in some woods. However, I don't think the added expense of carbide is worth the time and money. It's convenient to walk to the grinder and sharpen the HSS, and then walk back to the lathe and continue work.

After further consultation with turning friends, I realized that a smaller set of tools would be helpful. I purchased some 1/8" O-1 drill rod and some 1/16" HSS round material. While creating this set, I realized why machinists charge the rates they do. After quite a few missed drilling attempts trying to center this small of a hole, I made a trip to a local machine shop and paid the price to have the holes drilled properly. After a little more research, I discovered a smaller set of centering drills to start

the hole and a short drill bit used in drilling machines. You can purchase these from any machinist supply. A regular drill bit with the standard length has too much flex with the pressure that is needed to drill the hole. This shorter drill made life easier, so I purchased various sizes of shorter bits. (Because the center drills and bits occasionally break, keep a few spares on hand.)

These 1/8" cutting rods are cut shorter and I have made only two styles: a straight one and one curved for undercutting. I use only round HSS for the cutters in this size tool. To allow these to fit the same handle, I use 1/4"-diameter brass rod that I cut to approximately 1" in length and face the edges, then center-drill a 1/8" hole 3/4" deep. After heat-treating the drill rod, I glue the cutters in place, shape on the grinder and glue the 1/4" brass rod on to the drill rod.

To take these tools to another level, I came up with one final size. A professional turner who specializes in miniatures recommended 1/16" cutters fitted into a 1/4" brass rod. The material I use is 1/16" 0-1 drill rod, and so far I've only made a straight and a curved cutter.

Before gluing the cutter into the brass, I heat the drill rod to cherry red, which takes far less time than larger diameter drill rods. I again quench in the peanut oil. I made the

With the undercut tool Wayne hollows out a 2″ diameter vessel.

first batch without annealing and found the metal too hard and broke easily. I then began annealing them, which improved the performance. This is a synopsis of what I have learned through trial and error and I welcome your ideas on improving the miniature tools.

Wayne Fitch of Fort Worth, Texas, has found turning a beneficial method of stress relief after a 34-year career in law enforcement.

Make a Thin-Kerf Parting Tool

Stacey W. Hager

It was a dark and dreary midnight seven years past. (All good stories begin like this.) I was well into turning a lidded box with grain that promised to be a bear to match at the joint.

What I needed was a thin-kerf parting tool like the one I had watched Chris Stott use several months before. I began scrounging around my shop for something from which I might make a reasonable facsimile.

I found an old power hacksaw blade. With my metal chopsaw, I cut off one end at about 30 degrees.

I started to grind the edge and then remembered a sentence from the sharpening instructions packaged with my Oneway Wolverine jig. To paraphrase, laying the blade flat on the grinding platform (Figure H) produces a slight hollow grind (Figure C), which is ideal for clean parting. I found this advice difficult to follow with my regular diamond-profile parting tool, but why not try it here with this new thin parting tool?

It worked! In fact, it cut so cleanly, and so smoothly, and with so little effort that I regretted not having another person awake at 1 a.m. to watch as those delicate ribbons floated onto my forearm.

I have given these tools to friends and visiting demonstrators who have stayed at our home. Many say they use them regularly. Here's how to make one for yourself.

Choose a blade

Starrett, Ingersoll-Rand, Lenox, Disston-Porter, Borg-Warner, and Armstrong-Blum manufacture power hacksaw blades. Grainger (www.grainger.com) is one well-known catalog source. I've had good luck with high-speed steel blades, but you'll also find welded bi-metal and high-carbon steel blades. Dimensions range from 12" to 30" (length), 1" to 2-5/8" (width), .050" to 100" (thickness). For general use, I prefer 18" x 1-1/4" x .062".

I get free used blades from the welding department at my local community college. For ultra-thin kerfs (.027"), I prefer perforating blades from the printing industry. Zimmer Industries and Simonds, Inc. manufacture these high-carbon steel blades. Your local printers may discard used blades. Note: You'll need to add a handle on the printer blades, as the metal edge would cut into your palm.

AW 19:3, p18

Grind off the teeth

Because you can heat high-speed steel until dull-red without losing hardness, you can grind without concern for temper, as shown in *Figure A*. If you heat high-carbon steel much above the boiling point of water (212° F), you risk losing the ability to hold an edge. If carbon steel turns blue, you must carefully grind back to uncolored metal in order to find properly tempered steel.

Establish 30-degree angle

At a metal-cutting chopsaw, wedge or clamp the blade at the proper angle as shown in *Figure B*. (You may not be able to hold the blade firmly enough with just your hand.)

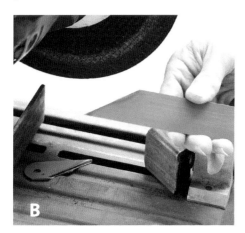

5 Advantages of a thin parting tool

- Thin kerf: The usual kerf is 1/16" (.062"). I made one ultra-thin parting tool that cuts a .020" kerf. This is ideal for lidded containers.

- Clean cutting: The points of the curved tip cut fibers before the center rakes out the chips, as shown in Figure C.

- Stability: The cutting tip is low on the tool. This eliminates the tendency to twist, which increases as you raise the center of force (cutting edge) above the level of the tool rest. Start parting with the parting tool horizontal or tilted slightly downward. This scraping start prevents "fuzzing-up" the beginning of the cut. Once started, drop the handle (which raises the tip) and "turn the tangent," as shown.

- Doubles as scraper: For cleaning up the surface in tight spaces, this tool also scrapes. Just tilt the blade a few degrees off vertical and into the work. The sharp edge of the hollow-ground angle will shear-scrape beautifully.

- Safety: The long handle gives enough leverage to prevent large forces from transmitting to the hand. If any parting tool begins to bind in the kerf, you should back out and widen the cut. You may choose to add a wooden handle to this tool.

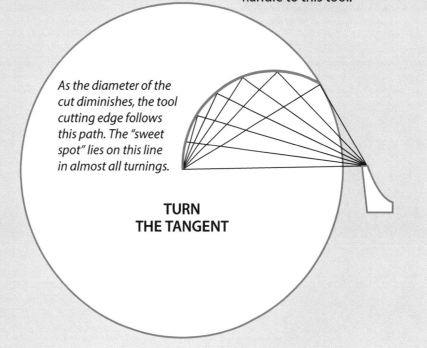

As the diameter of the cut diminishes, the tool cutting edge follows this path. The "sweet spot" lies on this line in almost all turnings.

TURN THE TANGENT

Round the handle

To prevent the corners from digging into your palm, gently cure the handle end of the parting tool as shown in *Figure D*.

Break the sharp edges

A hardened hollow-ground edge will destroy your tool rest rapidly. To avoid this, round the top and bottom edges of the blade slightly with a hone or sandpaper as shown in *Figure E*. Make the blade feel comfortable in your hand without completely destroying the flatness of the bottom edge.

Hollow-grind the major and micro bevels

Adjust the tool rest on your grinder so that the center of the rotation of the wheel passes through the center of your saw blade when it is extended over the tool rest past the grinder shaft as shown in *Figure F*. You can confirm this adjustment by hollow-grinding a section of the blade, then flipping it over and lightly touching the same edge to the wheel. Because the wheel should grind exactly the same curve when the blade is reversed, you should see no facets.

Adjust the tool rest by tapping with a small hammer as shown in

Figure G. Hollow-grind the major bevel as shown in Figure H. Then flip over the blade and form the micro bevel by lightly hollow-grinding the bottom edge of the tip at approximately 30 degrees. The micro bevel should be less than 1/16"—just enough to raise the cutting tip above the blunted bottom edge of the tool.

Stacey Hager is a member of the Central Texas Woodturners Association of Austin. He has been a frequent contributor to American Woodturner magazine.

Making Gouges

Ed French and John Shrader

It's a common belief that if you want high-speed steel turning gouges, you must buy them from manufacturers because the heat-treating is too difficult to make them in the wood turning shop.

We'd like to dispel that myth and show you a way to make your own high-speed steel gouges using worn out or surplus machine tools such as reamers and drills. The equipment required for the fabrication is common to most wood turning shops, or can be obtained easily and inexpensively. *Figure 1* shows typical gouges we've made by this technique.

The basic technique is to shape a grinding wheel to rough-grind the groove in a round piece of hardened high-speed steel, then to polish the groove with a wheel of MDF that has the groove shape impregnated with abrasive.

Find a source for scrap

The first step is to find a source of high-speed tool-steel. Machine shops, sharpening services, surplus stores, and mail-order houses for machine-shop supplies are all potential sources. *Figure 2* shows some typical surplus items that can be made into gouges. For this article, we purchased the raw material from Boeing Surplus in Seattle, WA. Our raw materials were mostly surplus reamers, but included drills with long shafts and hole saws. MSC Direct is one mail-order and Internet house that sells hardened drill blanks.

Figure 1: Gouges can be made from round rods of hardened high-speed steel by grinding and polishing the flute.

Figure 2: Used steel tools like these offer an inexpensive source of hardened steel suitable for home-made turning gouges.

AW 18:3, p25

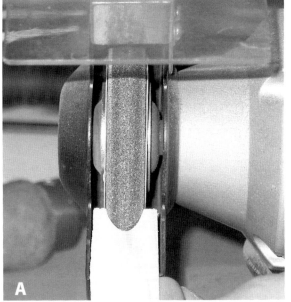

A

Use a template to verify the profile of the gouge.

B

With a wheel dresser, shape the grinding wheel to the gouge profile.

Choose your shape

The next step is to decide on the flute shape for the gouge. A few typical shapes are shown in *Figure 3*. Once the flute shape is decided, you must shape the grinding wheel to match the flute shape. It's helpful to make a female template for the grinding wheel out of thin material such as heavy cardboard or thin plywood as shown in *Figure 3*.

Shape a grinding wheel

The grinding wheel should be considered dedicated gouge-making, since converting it back to a standard sharpening shape will involve removing a lot of material.

The grinding wheel is then shaped using either a diamond wheel dresser or a star dresser as shown in *Figure B*. WARNING! It's very important to wear breathing, hearing, and eye protection during this process, as it produces a lot of grit and noise. The gray grinding wheels are cheaper and will hold their shape longer, but they also cut much slower than the white or pink wheels.

Grind the groove

The next step is to grind the groove in the piece of high-speed steel. Not all surplus tools are hardened for the full length of the shaft. A quick way to determine if the shaft is hardened

or not is to see if you can scratch it with a sharp cutting edge of another cutting tool. If you can scratch the shaft, it is not fully hardened.

Once the piece of steel has been selected, cut it so a smooth shaft is available for shaping into a gouge. After the initial groove is established, you can proceed with the grinding by just staying with the initial groove and gradually deepening it, as shown in Figure C. It is very much like riding the bevel when cutting wood on the lathe. Periodically, stop the grinding process and check the wheel profile using the template made earlier. If necessary, reshape the grinding wheel.

Polish the groove

When the rough shaping is completed, polish the groove using a wheel of MDF. This wheel is shaped the same as or a bit skinnier than the grinding wheel using the template for the grinding wheel to define the shape, as shown in Figure D. After shaping the wheel, impregnate it with 120-grit silicon carbide. The

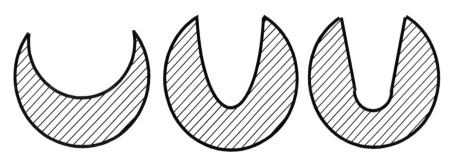

Figure 3: Decide the flute shape you want and make a female template.

C Gradually deepen and lengthen the groove to at least 1-1/2" long.

D E The MDF wheel, left, is slightly narrower for polishing, right.

silicon carbide grit is available at lapidary shops and auto supply stores. At machinist suppliers, you'll find this product as a lapping compound mixed in grease.

This step requires only a small amount of grit. The first layer of grit was applied by painting yellow glue on the outer edge of the MDF wheel, then sprinkling on a heavy layer of the grit before the glue dries. Repeat after the first layer of grit and glue dries. Subsequent layers were applied by mixing the grit in paste wax. You need to coat only the area of the wheel that matches the flute.

If the MDF wheel profile is the same as the grinding wheel profile, this step should go relatively quickly. You also can change the shape of the flute slightly at this stage, but this will take a long time, since very little metal is being removed at a time. This step also works for polishing commercial gouges, which do not always have smoothly polished grooves. Mount the MDF wheel on a bench grinder or your lathe. The wheel for this article was made 8" in diameter to match the regular sharpening wheels. *Figure E* shows the polishing step.

Give your gouge a grip

The gouge is now ready for a handle. Your handle could be a traditional straight wooden handle with the gouge either epoxied or driven in. Or try a handle made of aluminum or steel tubing with a set screw to hold different gouges. Some turners find a pistol-grip handle works best for some applications.

Shape and sharpen

Finally, you'll shape and sharpen the cutting edge as with any lathe tool at a regular grinding wheel.

Time for a few more?

Once you've made one gouge, you can create additional gouges using the same process for little more than the cost of the tool steel. By making your own gouges, you can try a variety of gouge shapes to closer match tasks and wood species.

To save fabrication time, you can grind a relatively short section of the groove to see if that shape is desirable. Works great? If so, lengthen the groove. If it is not, there is only a small time investment.

Ed French and John Shrader are members of the Seattle Chapter of the AAW.

Side-Ground Gouge

Phil Pratt

It's a question that novice and intermediate woodturners return to again and again as they reach various plateaus in their development. It's fundamental: Where does good technique begin? How does good technique become second nature, so that focus can shift toward form and expression?

Seven years ago I considered myself a better-than-average woodturner. I was beginning to understand why a poorly designed bowl would always be a clunker, even if it was turned from a dazzling piece of cherry or maple burl. It was easy to appreciate the seamless beauty of an Al Stirt platter or a John Jordan vessel. I wanted to share their knack for knowing just the right angle at which to turn the corner on a closed-form. In my own haphazard way, I was beginning to find myself as a woodturner, but I was still lacking the confidence in my technical skills from which I could reach the next level.

I remember vividly the day that David Ellsworth put a properly sharpened side-ground gouge in my hands. As I held the tool, he angled the cutting edge and helped me set those wispy ribbons of wood to flying. It was one of those rare moments of truth that raises the curtain on a whole new area of creative pursuit. Over the next few weeks, I spent many hours at the lathe developing confidence and predictability with this new tool. It took lots of practice to stabilize my technique at the grinder to reproduce the edge I wanted. Gradually, I began to understand how that long side grind was the focal point for proper tool manipulation and support.

Command of the side-ground gouge begins with your feet. The whole body, pivoting on the feet, moves the tool.

Here is what I learned: The feet become the pivot point for those smooth, flowing curves we all want in our work *(Figure 1)*. Shifting your weight from one foot to the other becomes the basis for good tool movement. The whole body must be involved in sweeping the tool through a long cut such as profile shaping or hollowing from rim to foot. Obviously, there are still many subtleties requiring the deft coordination of hand and eye. Some

twists and turns can be accomplished only at the tips of your fingers. But when it comes to realizing the side-grind's full potential for slicing, shearing, and shaping, the body must move the tool.

In order for this to happen, the gouge must be properly supported, and I have identified four basic points of tool support. The first three are rather obvious: the tool rest, the left hand, and the right hand. But the fourth point of support is every bit as important: except when hollowing, the handle of the gouge must maintain firm contact with your body, especially when the side-ground gouge is angled at 45 degrees for a smooth, slicing cut. I like to set the handle right at the opening of my pants pocket *(Figure 2)*. That usually means my right or left hand (depending on the direction of cut) is gripping the handle right below where the shaft emerges, allowing me to extend my index finger for extra support. The other hand becomes the manipulator, setting and adjusting the angle of cut, but also pushing the tool (often with the thumb) in the desired direction and keeping it firmly planted on the tool rest.

When a heavy gouge is used for initial roughing of a bowl blank, or it is necessary to flatten a spot for a faceplate or chuck fitting, then the tool must be held at a more-or-less horizontal angle. In this case, the handle can be supported under the forearm, and extra support is available (especially when roughing) by locking the handle between the forearm and torso *(Figure 3)*.

I find that even though the intended cut dictates which gouge

Photos by Dave Hillerby.

AW 12:1, p26

2

For a smooth, slicing cut, the tool handle must maintain firm contact with the body where your pants pocket opens.

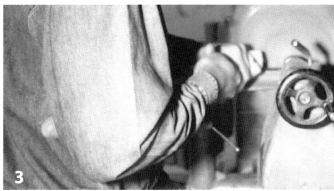

3

For initial roughing or flattening, when the tool is held more horizontal, lock the handle between your forearm and body.

I reach for, variations of the swept-back, side-grind have found their way onto most of the tools I use *(Figure 4)*. An extra-heavy super mega-flute gouge is my choice for the lumps and bumps of initial rough-out. Once the hard angles are smoothed out, I might switch to a 1/4-inch deep-fluted Glaser gouge with a shorter fingernail tip.

But, by far, my favorite tool is the Henry Taylor M-2 gouge with a long (up to 1-1/4 inch) side grind. The M-2, with its shallower flute, is clearly the tool of choice for subtle shaping cuts. I'm able to easily shift the gouge to either cutting edge, quickly reversing the direction of cut. I use the last quarter-inch near the tip to sweep away the high spots on a side profile that has warped as the bowl blank dried. I then use the edge further back on the side grind to slice the wood and re-define the bowl profile. Finally, I rotate the bevel off

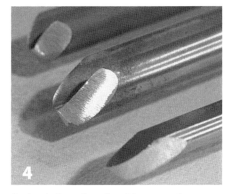

4

Author's three favorite side-ground gouges (from top to bottom): 3/4 in. Glaser, Super Mega-Flute, and Henry Taylor M-2 with extra-long side grind.

the wood, so that the edge alone is in contact, to shear-scrape the surface.

An important thing to remember is that the same methods of supporting the tool and moving the body at the lathe apply to the grinder as well. I like to hold the tool with my thumb on top and my index and middle finger underneath resting on the grinder's tool support *(Figure 5)*. The handle is locked between

my forearm and stomach. I present the tip of the gouge (flute up) to the grinding wheel at a 30-degree angle. Then, feet planted, I swing my body to the right, grinding the full length of the right bevel *(Figure 6)*. For the left bevel, I shift hands and swing to the left. Most importantly, I position the bevel on the wheel, from bottom to top (heel to edge), then grind in one, smooth sweep from the tip to the side of the tool. Don't focus on the cutting edge, or you'll end up with a rounded, misshapen bevel that will completely frustrate your ability to utilize the side-grind effectively.

Most woodturners experience an important breakthrough on the day their mastery of tool manipulation permits them to quit thinking about technique and start thinking about form and line and proportion. The side-grind can get you there faster.

Phil Pratt is a professional turner in Greensboro, NC.

5

Begin grinding the side-grind at the tip of the tool. Keep the handle tucked under your arm.

6

Concentrate on the bevel, not the edge, as you rotate your body and swing the tool to the side.

Making and Using a Hook Tool

Raul V. Pena

I like to turn small boxes, so I spend a lot of time hollowing out the end grain. I have used scrapers, gouges and ring tools with some success, but never came up with a technique that let me consistently turn a thin-walled box and finish the inside without much sanding.

Alan Lacer's rotations at recent symposiums convinced me the hook tool was the answer and gave me the confidence to try some basic blacksmithing.

I made dozens of hooks before I began to understand why hook tools give people so much grief.

The first thing that I learned is that it is imperative that the bevel stay in contact with the workpiece, once the cut is initiated (what most turners call rubbing the bevel).

The second thing was that it is important to understand the direction the wood moves with respect to the cutting edge. If we hold the cutting edge perpendicular to the tool rest, a hook tool will only cut if the tool is held below the level

If the shaving is too thick, and you experience noise and vibration, push the tool handle away from you to make a smaller shaving. The author recommends exerting only light pressure on the tool and running the lathe at 400 to 800 RPMs.

of the tool rest and below the center of rotation of the piece. Above this line the wood is moving from right to left and passing over the cutting edge from the back. Below this line the wood is moving from left to right and moving into the cutting edge. The best cutting area is a small pie-shaped area just below the center line

(Figure 2). If the tool is moved too far below this area, then the main force of the shaving will not push down on the tool rest, but it will push the tool sideways on the tool rest. If, however, you rotate the tool clockwise a few degrees (expose the cutting edge to the wood), you also rotate the optimal

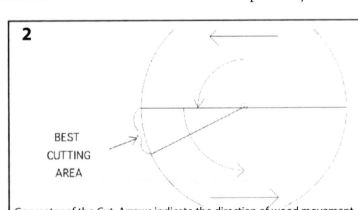

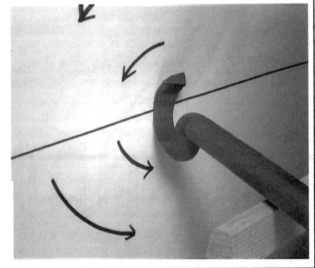

2 BEST CUTTING AREA

Geometry of the Cut. Arrows indicate the direction of wood movement as the blank spins; the most effective cutting area is slightly below center, where the wood moves into the edge. If the shaving is too thick, and you experience noise and vibration, push the tool handle away from you to make a smaller shaving. The author recommends exerting only light pressure on the tool and running the lathe at 400 to 800 RPMs.

Photos and drawings by the author.

AW 15:2, p24

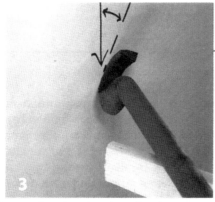

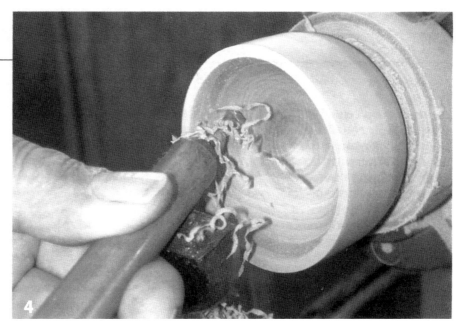

Figure 3. Rotating the edge a few degrees clockwise moves the optimal cutting area so the tool can cut along the centerline.

Figure 4: To move from the bottom up the side of a vessel, rotate the handle clockwise and push the handle away from you as you pull the tool up the wall. Keeping the angle between the cutting edge and the wood less than 45° generally is a good approach for most cuts.

cutting area so that the tool can cut effectively along the centerline.

Initiating the cut

To initiate a cut you begin near the center of rotation. Bring the bevel in contact with the wood, rotate the tool handle clockwise about 10° (expose the cutting edge to the wood), tilt the handle toward you (increase the clearance angle or the distance from the bottom of the cutting edge to the wood) while pulling the tool toward you, then tilt the handle away from you to control the thickness of the shaving. If you want a flat bottom: pull the tool toward you while keeping the angle of the tool handle constant. If the shaving is too thick then you will

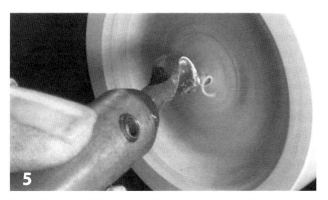

Rotate the tool 180° so the cutting edge points to the center of rotation to remove the center nub.

experience some noise and vibration. Minimize this by pushing the tool handle away from you to make a smaller shaving *(Figure 1)*.

As you get farther from the center, you may have to rotate the shaft of the tool clockwise a little to eliminate vibration caused by the changing angle of the wood meeting the cutting edge. If you want a round bottom or a curve from a flat bottom to the side, rotate the handle of the tool clockwise and push the handle away from you while you pull the tool up the side of the vessel, as shown in Figure 4. Both of these moves will decrease the clearance angle, which allows you to cut curved surfaces or change the direction of the cut. The comfort level of the position determines the amount of each move that you make. The important thing is to keep the bevel in contact with the wood during the transition from bottom to side.

The bump on the bottom that forms at the center of rotation can be removed easily by rotating the tool 180° so that the cutting edge points

to the center of rotation, as shown in Figure 5. Bring the bevel in contact with the work along the centerline and open the face of the tool by rotating the tool counter-clockwise a few degrees. Now make small cuts by moving the tool toward the center until the high spot is removed or a slight concave shape is achieved. Rotate the tool back to the normal position and make a final cut to smooth the transition between the two cuts, as previously described.

One reason people have trouble with hook tools is that they expect them to act like bowl gouges. The basic difference is that as we cut from the lip of the vessel to the bottom, the shavings are pushing the gouge against the inside wall of the vessel and down on the tool rest. The vessel wall keeps the gouge from sliding sideways off the tool rest.

On the hook tool the forces are rotated by 90°. The bevel is still keeping the tool in place but that force is along the tool shaft and the bevel is the only thing preventing the shavings from pulling the tool out of your hand. That's why riding the bevel is so important.

Developing my own design

My original hook for cutting a flat bottom, *Figure 6*, was more aggressive than my tool for shaping the sides. That's because there are two ways of increasing the clearance angle. The first is to rotate the handle toward you so that the tool is no longer perpendicular to the cutting surface (a small clearance angle). This is in fact a good way to initiate the cut, but you must rotate the tool handle back perpendicular to the cutting surface or the tool will dig into the work. You can also increase the clearance angle by rotating the shaft clockwise a few degrees and tilting the handle up slightly. This move can often lead to a catch.

My tool for shaping the sides, *Figure 7*, is more user-friendly: it has only one way to increase the clearance angle—by pulling the handle toward you. If you rotate the shaft of this tool clockwise, the bevel pushes the cutting edge away from the inside of the bowl and decreases the clearance angle. If you rotate the tool counter-clockwise, you increase the clearance angle but you also move the cutting edge into a more neutral cutting position (cutting edge parallel to the wood movement) and this rarely leads to a catch.

Since I couldn't make a flat bottom with this tool, I decided to forge a hook tool that had characteristics of both of my tools— user friendly and able to cut both flats and curves. On the combination grind I developed, the cutting edge is on the inside of the hook, like the side cutting hook, but the bevel angle varies from about 10° at the tip to about 45°. This tool, shown in *Figure 8*, will not cut when held with the shaft perpendicular to the work surface. The handle must be tilted about 10° toward you for the cutting edge to contact the wood. If you raise the handle or if you rotate the shaft of the tool clockwise more than 20°, the cutting edge will be lifted from the work piece (decrease the clearance angle). Once the bevel

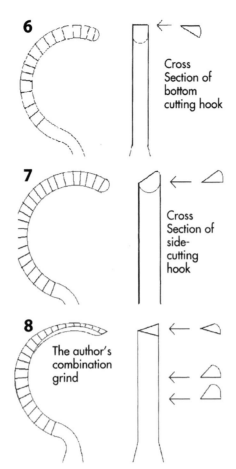

6 Cross Section of bottom cutting hook

7 Cross Section of side-cutting hook

8 The author's combination grind

is in contact with the surface, you can control the cutting by moving the handle toward you. In order to shape the sides, simply rotate the shaft of the tool clockwise and swing the tool handle away from you while you pull the tool up the side of the vessel. It is possible to make a transition from the bottom to the side by rotating the tool clockwise and swinging the tool handle away from you in one smooth move. You can control how aggressively the tool cuts by swinging the tool handle in or out. The important thing to remember is to always keep the bevel in contact with the wood and the angle between the cutting edge and the wood rotation less than 45°. By rotating the shaft of the tool and swinging the handle toward you or away from you, you can easily control this. The real safety feature of this tool is that it is not possible to rotate the tool shaft clockwise 90° and keep the cutting edge on the wood, if you keep the tool

handle close to parallel to the floor. (This maneuver will generally lead to a catch with a bottom-cutting tool or a ring tool.)

Filing a hook
Hook tools must be very sharp, or they will be hard to use and will tear the end grain. I sharpen my tools with a fine diamond rat-tail file. I always give a tool a few strokes with the file before using it and test for sharpness by lightly touching the cutting edge on my fingernail. If the tool slides on your fingernail, it needs sharpening. If the edge catches on your nail, it is sharp. If I feel resistance in cutting, I test the sharpness and resharpen.

Making a hook tool
Forming a hook tool is simple, as shown in *Figure 9*.

1. Start with Ol (oil-hardening) drill rod (1/4 in. to 3/8 in. diameter).

2. Grind the two sides flat about 1 inch back from the tip to form a tang. With 1/4 in. stock grind to about a thickness of 3/16 in.

3. Heat the end with a Mapp gas or acetylene torch until it glows with a deep orange color. Bend it into a J shape using needle-nose pliers.

4. Reheat the hook and bend at the base of the curve to form the shape of a question mark. At this point it may be necessary to shape the inside to a round shape of either 1/4 or 3/8 in. This is done by placing a hardened steel bolt or rod in a vise, heating the hook and placing the hook around the bolt, and lightly tapping it with a small hammer. Repeat the process until the desired "?" shape is achieved.

5. Reheat the hook and twist the hook end a little, as shown in step 5 of *Figure 9*.

Grinding the bevel
Grind the bevel by holding the tool parallel to the floor and tilted at a

slight angle (about 10°). As you grind, hold the tool in this position while you rotate the shaft clockwise to about 20°. Continue this routine until the bevel has almost been ground to the inside edge of the hook. There will remain material from the point where you have been grinding to the tip of the hook that can be removed simply by lifting up on the shaft to form a smooth rounded curve to the end of the hook. Be sure to maintain the 10-degree angle from perpendicular while removing excess material.

Next, start with the tool parallel to the floor with the shaft tilted 10 degrees from the perpendicular and rotated clockwise 20 degrees. Begin grinding while rotating the tool to about 45 degrees and swinging the tool to the left to about 50 or 60 degrees. Try to make a continuous smooth bevel through this arc. Repeat until the bevel almost reaches the inside of the hook.

Finally, use a flat file to smooth any imperfections in the bevel and a round file to clean up the inside of the hook. At this point the inside of the hook and the bevel should meet to make a knife edge.

The tool should have the profiles shown in *Figures 6, 7 and 8* when the rough shaping is finished. The cross section at the tip of the tool should make about a 10° angle from the perpendicular. The side of the hook (a point 90° from the tip of the tool) should make about a 45° angle from the perpendicular. Grind the outer edge of the hook until the bevel is about 1/8 in. from the cutting edge to the non-cutting edge. Since the bevel is so important, it is critical that its non-cutting edge be rounded and polished so that it won't scratch a curved surface.

Heat treating

Before heat treating the hook tool, use a hack saw and cut a groove around the drill rod at the point

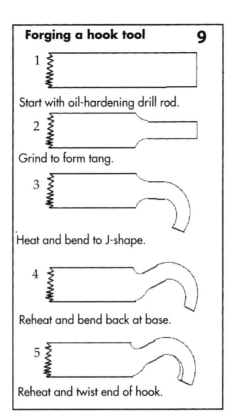

Forging a hook tool 9

1. Start with oil-hardening drill rod.

2. Grind to form tang.

3. Heat and bend to J-shape.

4. Reheat and bend back at base.

5. Reheat and twist end of hook.

that will be the final length of the tip, about 1-3/4 in. Leave a small piece of metal connecting the tip and the rod. After heat treating and sharpening it will be easy to break off the tip. Also grind a flat spot near the end of the tool that fits into your tool holder for the set-screw to hold the tip securely. The flat ground spot should be on the same side as the sharp edge of the hook tool. This will keep the set-screw away from the tool rest while you are using the tool.

Heat the rod with a MAPP gas or an acetylene torch and let the temperature slowly move up the rod until the tip loses its magnetic property. Test the tip with a magnet until there is no sign of magnetism.

Plunge the rod into an oil container and move it as if you were stirring a pot. Boiled linseed oil or olive oil work fine. Use a fireproof metal can for the quenching oil.

Break the tip from the rod and place the hook tool in an oven, a barbeque grill, or in a deep fryer set at 300° F, for about 10 minutes. This will temper the tip to a hardness (and

toughness) of 63-65 R.C. The tool is ready to be sharpened and used.

Sharpening

Mount your hook tool in your tool holder or clamp it in a vise. Begin by making sure that the bevel is either flat or slightly hollow ground. Use a sharpening stone or a diamond file to clean up any imperfections in the bevel surface. Round off and polish any sharp edges on the non-cutting edge of the bevel.

After the bevel has been ground, hone the inside of the hook tool with a round diamond file until a sharp edge develops. Create a small micro-bevel by sharpening at a slightly steeper angle than the inside of the hook.

Congratulations, you are finished and are ready to use the tool. This tool should make a nearly glass-like smooth cut that requires little or no sanding. If you feel torn fibers, check to make sure that you have a flat bevel (no rounding at the cutting edge) and a sharp edge.

Tool holder

A tool holder can be made by drilling a 1/4-in. (or 3/8-in.) hole in the end of a 5/8-inch mild steel rod (either cold roll or hot roll will work). The cadmium plated round steel bars available at most hardware stores in 3-foot lengths work just fine. Drill a small hole about 1/2 to 3/4 in. back from the end of the bar and tap it to accept a set-screw. Turn a tool handle from some scrap hardwood and make a tenon to fit a ferrule made from a piece of pipe or tubing (copper, brass, iron or stainless steel all work fine). Drill a 5/8-in. hole in the end of the tenon and epoxy your rod into the tool handle.

You're ready to turn.

Raul Pena is a turner in Camp Verde, TX and an active member of the Hill Country Turners chapter of the AAW.

Texture Tool

Bob Rosand

Two of the great benefits of demonstrating at chapters around the country are that demonstrators get to show members how they turn and learn from others—if they keep their eyes and ears open.

About a year ago, I visited the Ohio Valley Woodturner Guild. Before the weekend was over, I spent several hours in John Lannom's shop. John has a great shop and turns some wonderful work, but the thing that caught my eye was a wide-rimmed platter that had some very nice "orange peel" texturing. I commented that the texturing must have been time-consuming. John's response was that it took only four or five minutes to texture the surface.

Using the technique he learned from Trent Bosch, John textured his platter with a needle scaler. This is an impact tool that welders rely on to remove scale from welds. The scaler requires about 90 pounds of air pressure to operate properly.

I'm having fun with my own scaler and since buying it, I've textured lidded boxes, tool handles, oil lamps, paperweights, platters, and bowls. Here are two projects that show off these texturing techniques.

A needle scaler driven by compressed air makes a great texturing tool for woodturning.

1

Oil lamp

Select a 4 × 4 × 2" square of maple burl or other suitable turning stock. After mounting it in a scroll chuck, drill a 3/4"-deep hole with a 1-1/2"-diameter Forstner bit. (Verify the diameter with a tea candle or confetti candle purchased at a grocery store or crafts store.)

As you shape the body with a 3/8" spindle gouge, leave the shoulder square. You will later turn down the shoulder, but leave it in place for now so you can texture the body without affecting the final surface.

Turn off the lathe and begin texturing with the needle scaler. Apply light pressure and keep the tool moving. Note that the tool is positioned about 90 degrees to the work. It doesn't matter if the needles hit the squared neck of the oil lamp because you will turn away that section later.

To remove stray tool marks, turn the shoulder with a sharp square-nosed scraper. Create separation between the neck of the lamp and the body by cutting a V-groove with a small spindle gouge sharpened to a razor point.

Photos by the author.

2

The scaling tool made the texture on this oil lamp.

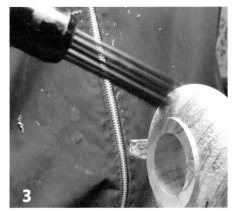

3

Because the shoulder will be contoured later, you can texture right up to the neck.

4

You can steady the bowl with one hand while you texture the oil-lamp surface.

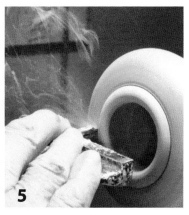

5

Use a small spindle gouge to separate the neck and body.

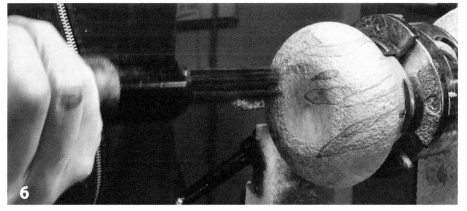

6

After turning the base of your oil lamp, texture the bottom with the needle scaler. Note how the tool is held at 90 degrees to the surface.

To turn the base, part the oil lamp from the lathe. Remount the piece on a friction-fit waste block. Then turn a slightly concave base. When you're satisfied with the shape, texture the base as previously described.

To finish your lamp, rub it with 0000 steel wool or synthetic steel wool saturated with walnut oil or a tung-oil product. If you apply a tung-oil, add a coat of paste wax, then buff.

Your next texturing device

The scaler is an impact tool. Air drives a small piston that randomly drives the gun's needles in and out, which marks the work.

From the factory, the needles are blunt. The first thing I did when my scaler arrived was to disassemble the scaler, remove each needle, and round over the tips on my grinder. Then I clamped each needle in a three-jaw chuck and sanded them smooth. After reassembly, I was ready to work.

The needle scaler requires little maintenance. It does require periodic lubrication (a couple of drops of oil before each use), but so far, I have yet to break a needle.

After you use it for a while, you will begin to notice little black specks appearing on your work. These are bits of old lubricant and dirt. When this happens, remove the needles, clean them and the scaler interior, and reassemble.

There are numerous needle scalers on the market, but some of them are cumbersome for this type of detail work. The scaler shown is a Sioux Falls mini-needle scaler. It has 12 needles and is relatively compact. I've talked to some people who found them for about $75 on the Internet. I've talked to some turners who purchased larger, cheaper scalers and they found them heavy and difficult to use.

This is one of the few tools that will to some extent hide shoddy workmanship. If you have some very minimal surface flaws they will in all probability disappear, but larger tear-outs and flaws will definitely be noticeable. If your tool control is good, you can probably get away with not sanding the piece before scaling the surface.

The scaler works best on end grain because you are impacting or pushing down the end-grain fibers. It also works well on side grain, but the scaler markings are not quite as distinguishable or precise.

The down side to this tool is that the random needle marks are hard to control and may wander into an area you don't want textured, like the neck of the oil lamp. Planning avoids this problem.

When you use the tool, hold it at about 90 degrees to the surface. If you don't, it will tend to skid off the surface. Apply a little downward pressure and keep the tool moving.

The texturing will be more defined if you leave the piece chucked while you texture it or leave it between centers like when texturing a tool handle. The results will be far better than if you try to hold the piece in your hand while texturing.

Bob Rosand of Bloomsburg, Pennsylvania, is a professional turner and educator and frequent contributor to American Woodturner.

Tool handle

Turning a handle for a lathe tool is a simple project that illustrates some of the effects you can get with the needle scaler.

With a roughing-out gouge, turn the handle shape from a 1-1/2 × 1-1/2 × 10" blank. (Cherry is shown in these how-to photos.)

At one end, turn and fit a ferrule from a piece of 1/2 × 1/2" copper tubing. Then, finish shaping the tool handle with a 1/2" skew.

Now, texture the surface with the needle scaler. Apply downward pressure and keep the tool moving. You will need to occasionally tighten the tailstock because the vibration of the scaler may loosen the mounting.

Texture the end of the tool, being sure to keep the scaler at about 90 degrees in relation to the area being textured. The lower handle in *Figure 7* shows four decorative lines cut into the handle. You may finish the handle at this point with walnut oil or tung oil.

For an aged appearance, apply a coat of black water-based milk paint, which dries fast, is durable, and sands off easily. The milk paint also darkens and ages the cherry. When you sand off the paint, you'll have three color layers: black paint, the darkened cherry, and a lighter layer of freshly exposed cherry.

After sanding with 220, 320, and 400 grits, apply the finish of your choice.

Tool handles are a good testing ground for the texturing tool.

7

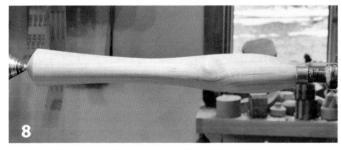

8

Establish the shape of your lathe-tool handle and fit a copper ferrule to the tenon end.

9

Hold the needle scaler at 90 degrees to the piece while you texture the entire length of the handle.

10

Apply a coat of black water-based milk paint to the handle, then allow to dry.

11

Sand high spots of the handle with 220-, 320- and 400-grit sandpaper. This reveals three color tones.

Golden Dividers

Bill Smith

Mathematicians, philosophers, and scientists studied it. Architects and engineers relied on it from ancient times to present day. Even Mother Nature likes it. And certainly all self-respecting artists—woodturners included—incorporate it in some form in a portion of their work.

I'm talking about the Golden Mean, that seemingly magical ratio of width to height that appeals to the eyes of so many.

Using the full-size patterns shown in *Figure 3*, you can easily incorporate the Golden Mean into your woodturning designs and see the correct 1:1.618 ratio at a glance.

Make your own dividers

The attached drawing was designed for turnings up to about 8". To make a larger set of dividers, scale up the drawings with an enlarging copy machine.

First, make a photocopy of the patterns. Using a spray adhesive (3M no. 77 adhesive works well), attach the patterns to a piece of 1/8"-thick acrylic plastic, metal, or another suitable substrate.

Cut out along the pattern lines with a scrollsaw or bandsaw. Be careful at the tips of the four arrows as they delineate the ratio—you want the divider profiles to just touch the arrow tips. (I hand-sand this area.) To protect the paper, apply two or three

coats of clear sealer such as Deft or Krylon.

Then drill a 5/32"-diameter hole for a #8×1/2" panhead machine screw and wing nut. To get an accurate set of dividers, you must drill carefully at the point marked with an "X." After assembly, the ultimate test is to close the dividers—the arrow tips should just touch.

Bill Smith is a woodturner from Doylestown, Pennsylvania.

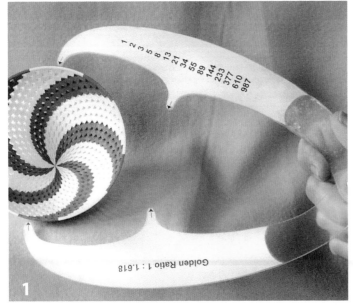

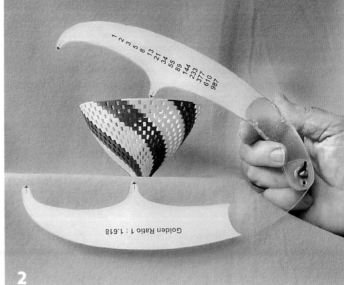

Put your Golden Dividers to work

This 2-3/4" x 4-1/2" bowl follows the 1:1.618 Golden Mean formula. The 4-1/2" width (Figure 1) matches the Golden Mean for the height (Figure 2).

AW 20:2, p14

1:1.618: Golden for 8 centuries

The ancients probably adopted the 1:1.618 ratio because it made things look good. In the thirteenth century, Italian mathematician Leonardo Fibonacci recognized a series of numbers that is now known as the Fibonacci series. As it turns out, if you divide any Fibonacci number by the previous number you get a close approximation of the Golden Mean. The series may be calculated by adding the previous number to the current number to get the next number (1 + 2 = 3, 2 + 3 = 5, 3 + 5 = 8 and so forth.

The Golden Mean has several uses in woodturning:

- While turning an object, adjust the height to the diameter.

- Divide a turning so that the lower section is 1.618 times the height of the top section.

- Divide a lidded box from top to bottom by the Golden Mean (the longer dimension is usually on the bottom).

The Golden Mean—while useful—is only a guide to one set of height and diameter ratios. If you rely on it too frequently your work will probably become boring. (At best, the Golden Mean figures into less than 20 percent of my own work.) There are many other shapes and ratios that work well. It is most important to make turnings that look good to your eye and have shapes that feel good to your touch.

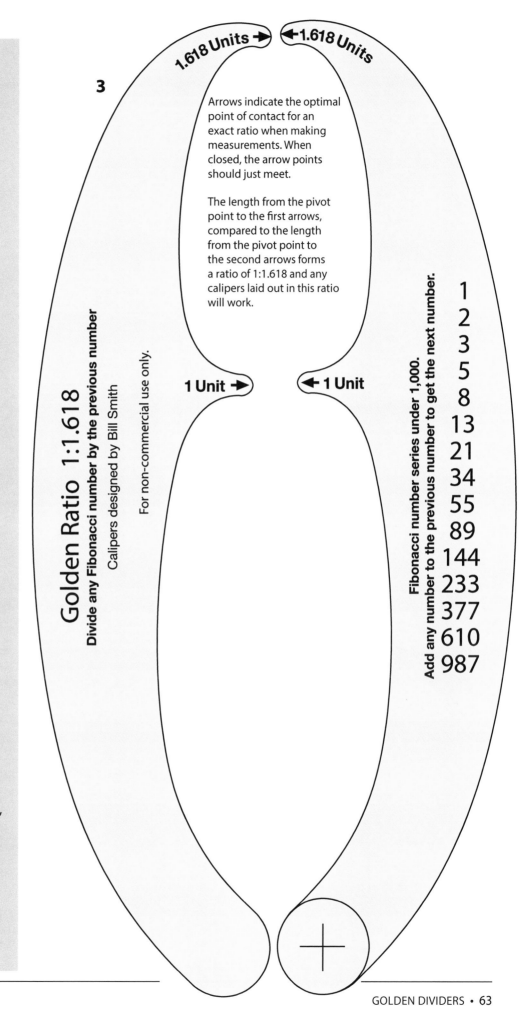

3

1.618 Units → ← **1.618 Units**

Arrows indicate the optimal point of contact for an exact ratio when making measurements. When closed, the arrow points should just meet.

The length from the pivot point to the first arrows, compared to the length from the pivot point to the second arrows forms a ratio of 1:1.618 and any calipers laid out in this ratio will work.

1 Unit → ← **1 Unit**

Golden Ratio 1:1.618
Divide any Fibonacci number by the previous number

Calipers designed by Bill Smith

For non-commercial use only.

Fibonacci number series under 1,000.
Add any number to the previous number to get the next number.

1
2
3
5
8
13
21
34
55
89
144
233
377
610
987